CLASSIC THUNDERBIRDS™

SECRET FILES

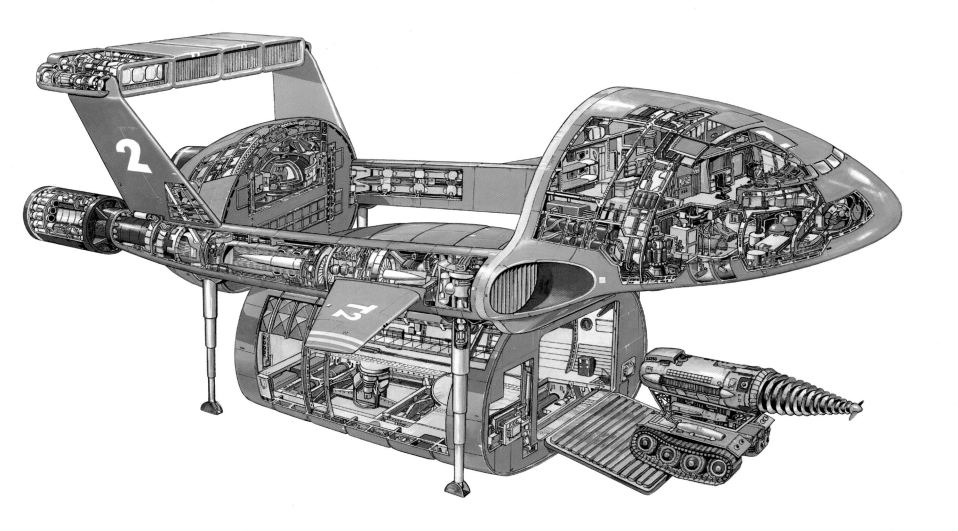

THE INSIDE STORY OF
INTERNATIONAL RESCUE

BY CHRIS BENTLEY, GRAHAM BLEATHMAN AND STEPHEN COLE

CARLTON
BOOKS

CONTENTS

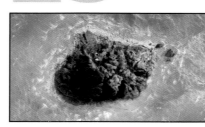

THIS IS A CARLTON BOOK

Published by Carlton Books Limited
20 Mortimer Street
London
W1T 3JW

ISBN 1 84442 977 6

Illustrations, text and design © 2000, 2003 Carlton Books Limited

™ and © 1964, 1999 and 2003.
THUNDERBIRDS is a Gerry Anderson Production.
Licensed by Carlton International Media Limited.

1 3 5 7 9 10 8 6 4 2

Printed in Singapore

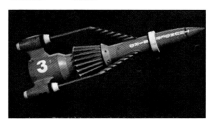

THE WORLD OF 2065

GLOBAL EVENTS IN THE LATTER HALF OF THE CENTURY

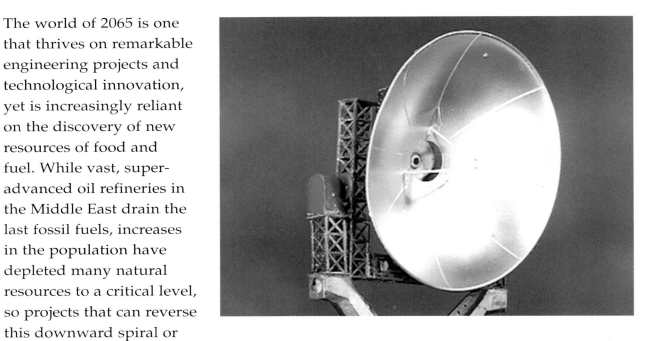

The world of 2065 is one that thrives on remarkable engineering projects and technological innovation, yet is increasingly reliant on the discovery of new resources of food and fuel. While vast, super-advanced oil refineries in the Middle East drain the last fossil fuels, increases in the population have depleted many natural resources to a critical level, so projects that can reverse this downward spiral or minimise further environmental damage have become of paramount importance.

RIGHT: A revolutionary solar generator designed by Professor Lungren can power an entire town.

BELOW: Super-fast and affordable air travel makes for a small world.

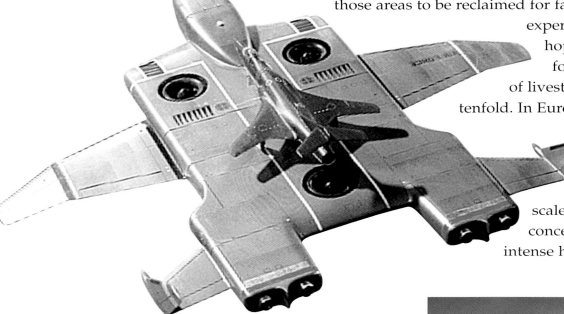

In the Australian Outback and the Sahara Desert, irrigation stations are being constructed that will use atomic reactors to pump sea water into the desert, enabling those areas to be reclaimed for farming. In South America, scientists experimenting with the drug theramine hope to provide a solution for the world food shortage by stimulating the growth of livestock, which could increase meat output tenfold. In Europe, experiments with cyclonic generators promise to be able to process solar radiation into electricity, solving the problem of storing electricity on a commercial scale by using cyclonic batteries to concentrate sunlight into a beam of intense heat and thereby generate power.

RIGHT: One of the biggest oil refineries in the Middle East, the A'Ben Duh installation.

Population growth has also meant that builders and architects need to look at more economic use of land for housing, with one solution being multi-level accommodation. The newly completed Thompson Tower maxi mall on America's west coast is a completely self-contained city, with every single commercial item produced throughout the entire world available on its 350 floors. It stands half a mile wide and

RIGHT: *Supported by a huge gantry tractor, the Empire State Building is shifting to a new location in 2065.*

BELOW: *A person could live for years in the rooms of the twelve hotels housed in the remarkable Thompson Tower – every service and facility necessary is provided.*

2 miles deep. Beneath the structure is a massive sub-basement that has parking for 10,000 cars and is linked to the store by a monorail 4 miles long.

The city of New York, on the other hand, has embarked on a long-term programme of redevelopment which involves an expensive and ingenious scheme to preserve the Empire State Building by moving it 200 yards to a new site. Ten years of planning and two years of construction have gone into the operation, all to enable the surrounding area to be completely redeveloped.

THE SPEED OF PROGRESS

THE FASTEST, THE BIGGEST, THE BEST

ABOVE: *The Paris–Anderbad Express is a stylish way to travel.*

By 2065 saturation road usage has been resolved by the development of more economic and efficient public transport. Many cities around the world, including London, Paris and New York, have replaced their old subway systems with overhead monorails, and monorail is also the transport service of choice for many transcontinental services, such as the coast-to-coast Pacific–Atlantic monorail which crosses the United States, and the Paris–Anderbad monorail through the Alps.

RIGHT: *Explosives tractors are used to blast away dangerous obstacles, clearing the way for new roads.*

Motorways and autobahns have largely been replaced by multi-lane superhighways such as the Great North–South Superhighway constructed in Britain in the early 2020s, and the more recent M104, still under construction. Roads such as these can now be completed at incredible speed using massive Road Construction Vehicles which flatten the ground in the path of the road, lay tarmac and paint lane markings all in a single pass. Similar vehicles are used to clear heavily forested regions for urban development or road construction. The Crablogger felling vehicle uses forward-mounted grabs on telescopic arms to cut down trees and feed them into a pulping machine. (See page 46).

RIGHT: *The Crablogger in action.*

Air travel has become more efficient and extensive, principally through the introduction of Air Terrainean's fleet of Fireflash atomic-powered passenger aircraft. Capable of flying at six times the speed of sound, the Fireflash carries 600 passengers at a height of 150,000 feet to destinations around the globe, including Tokyo, San Francisco, New York and Nice. The most aerodynamic vehicle yet created, the Fireflash's pencil-slim design relocates the pilot's cockpit to the rear tailfin, which is mounted by an elevated tailplane housing six atomic engines. These engines will, in principle, enable the craft to stay in the air for up to six months at a time, although the anti-radiation shielding on the reactor requires regular servicing.

BELOW: *A Fireflash arrives at New York Central Airport.*

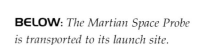

ABOVE: *The atomic-powered Fireflash shortly after take-off.*

Space exploration continues to be high on the agenda in the search for new resources, as projects to investigate other planetary bodies in the solar system will, it is hoped, have a beneficial impact back on Earth. One plan is to launch two astronauts aboard a Martian Space Probe rocket from a suitable launch site in Britain to undertake a scientific mission on the red planet.

Equally important is the Operation Sun Probe project, a manned mission to capture matter from the Sun by sending a probe capsule into a solar prominence. The launch of the Sun Probe rocket will rely on a new process which converts sea water into rocket fuel capable of exerting 20 million pounds of thrust.

BELOW: *The Martian Space Probe is transported to its launch site.*

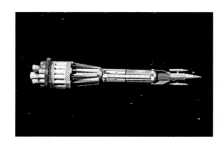

LEFT: *The Sun Probe, designed to collect solar matter for scientific research.*

A WORLD OF DANGER

WHY WE NEED INTERNATIONAL RESCUE

ABOVE: *Thunderbird 1 is usually first on the scene at any danger zone.*

Despite these incredible advances in design, human error and outside interference can still have a disastrous effect on new technology – and when this occurs, given the scale of many of the projects in operation around the globe, the results can be devastating. For in one area the world of 2065 is sorely lacking, and that is in the development by the authorities of suitable rescue machines and equipment to cope with the kind of disasters that are now possible. This imbalance has been redressed by the formation of an independent privately funded organization: International Rescue.

International Rescue's function is to act on any emergency call to assist in situations where conventional rescue methods have proved inadequate. At times, the organization may also choose to involve itself in operations which will ultimately save lives by preventing disaster situations before they arise. With an amazing array of rescue craft at their disposal – known as the

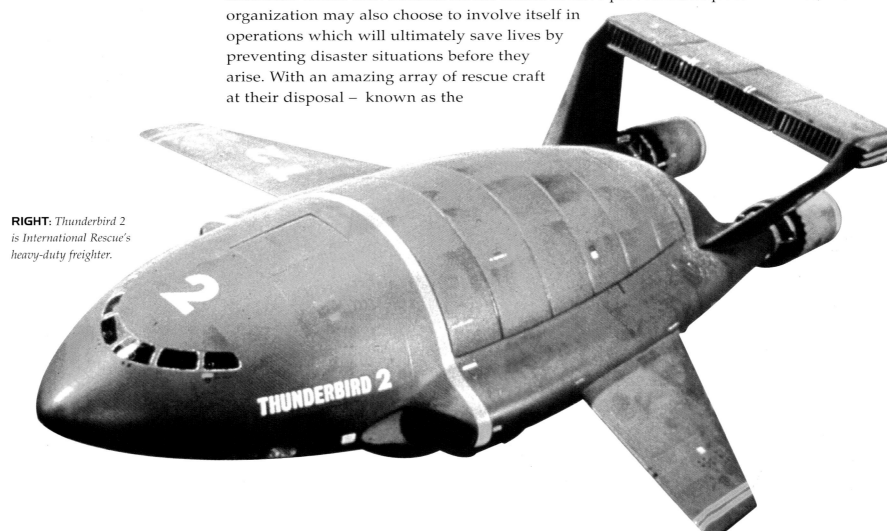

RIGHT: *Thunderbird 2 is International Rescue's heavy-duty freighter.*

Thunderbirds – International Rescue makes the world a safer place. Thunderbirds 1 to 4 are designed for active use in the danger zone, while Thunderbird 5 is an enormous communications satellite orbiting the Earth. The motto of International Rescue is 'Not to give up at any cost' and each of the organization's agents must be prepared to sacrifice his or her own life if doing so would save the lives of others.

Being privately funded and not in the control of any world power, International Rescue is able to operate freely to help anyone in distress, regardless of their politics or nationality. But to retain its independence, it must remain

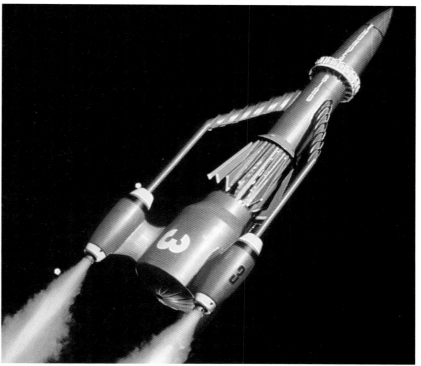

top secret at all times. International Rescue's vehicles and rescue machinery, designed by the mega-genius Brains, are probably more advanced than anything else on the planet. Certain special components were assembled in secret at factories and foundries in Europe – though what purpose they would ultimately be put to was withheld from the manufacturers – and the designs and specifications must be closely guarded. For even in this amazing futuristic world, there lingers still the traditional danger of crime and sabotage. Secrecy is vital in the world of 2065, since nothing – whether it be a revolutionary new fabric, some fearsome new military vehicle, or even the Thunderbird vehicles themselves – is safe from the evil ambitions of greedy crooks or bitter rivals.

TOP: *Thunderbird 3 is designed for space rescues.*

ABOVE LEFT: *Thunderbird 4 is a one-man submarine that tackles aquatic dangers.*

LEFT: *Watching over the Earth... Thunderbird 5 monitors constantly for distress signals in any language.*

CRIME UNLIMITED

THE PEOPLE WHO KEEP IR BUSY

It's not just unlucky accidents that can create dangerous situations for International Rescue – often a human hand is at work, so secrecy and security are important at all times. In its time, the organization has come up against thieves, saboteurs, hijackers and deadly villains… Here are just a few of them.

JENKINS AND CORELLA

CRIMES: Theft, international espionage, criminal deception

These crooks had an audacious plan – to impersonate the boys from International Rescue as a front for performing acts of espionage! The crooked duo rescued a man from an underground well and made off with the top-secret plans of the AL4, stolen from the nearby Aeronautical Centre.

When the robbery was discovered, a worldwide search was launched to track down International Rescue and bring them to justice – and that meant that the boys couldn't perform any real rescues without giving away their secret base! Luckily, International Rescue's network of secret agents was able to track down the imposters and bring them to justice.

DR GODBER

CRIMES: Kidnapping, blackmail, attempted murder

The evil Dr Godber would stop at nothing to get the secret formula of a revolutionary rocket fuel produced from sea water. He kidnapped Professor Borender, one of the inventors of the new fuel, from a monotrain and held him captive in the hope he could extract the information.

When International Rescue agents Lady Penelope and Sir Jeremy Hodge – who was Borender's partner – investigated the professor's disappearance, Dr Godber almost succeeded in killing them! Eventually he kidnapped them too and tried to blackmail the fuel's creators into revealing the secret process – by placing Lady Penelope directly in front of a speeding monotrain! Fortunately, the Tracy brothers were able to avert disaster.

THE ERDMAN GANG

CRIMES: Kidnapping, attempted murder, international sabotage

This criminal organization had a most unpleasant gimmick – they would strap exploding bracelets made from hydrochromatized steel to helpless people and so force them to carry out acts of sabotage. One such act brought about the destruction of extensive files on several criminal organizations, and another job was planned that would allow the Erdman gang to break into a plutonium storage facility. Eventually, Lady Penelope and Parker were able to bring down the gang's helijet with FAB 1's cannon.

GENERAL BRON

CRIMES: Paymaster for saboteurs

The sinister General Bron was a ruthless individual who would stop at nothing to ensure that his new and deadly fighter plane was the fastest and most vicious weapon in the sky. He hired the Hood to sabotage the new Red Arrow fighter plane, and sure enough the plane crashed into its launch site during its test flight.

World Space Control soon prepared red Arrow 2 for testing. The Hood was able to sabotage that flight too, but International Rescue exposed him and set the police on his tail. General Bron's evil ambitions were ultimately thwarted, as the Red Arrow test programme continued successfully – but this villain is still at large.

THE CHARACTERS

JEFF TRACY

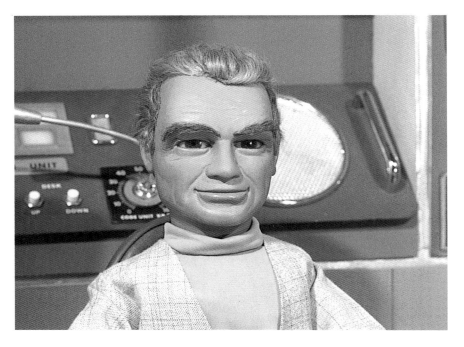

The patriarch of the Tracy family and founder of International Rescue, Jeff Tracy was born on 2 January 2009, the son of a Kansas wheat farmer. A colonel in the US Air Force before transferring to the Space Agency, Jeff counts himself among the first astronauts to land on the Moon during the early days of colonization. He abandoned his space career to raise his five sons after the tragic early death of his wife.

Entrepreneurial, spirited and adventurous, Jeff's genius for civil and construction engineering soon made him one of the richest men in the world, giving him the ability to finance International Rescue. He was inspired to form the organization after reading a report of a tragic air crash in which eighty people died, largely owing to inadequate rescue equipment and craft. Within two years, he had transformed his dream into reality.

Intelligent, kind and with a sense of humour, Jeff also exhibits the ability to be decisive and stern when the situation demands. Now fifty-six, Jeff is absolutely dedicated to the goals of International Rescue and rarely allows himself the luxury of time off from his duties.

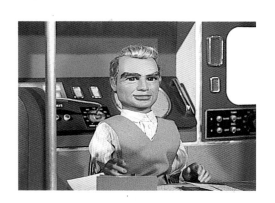

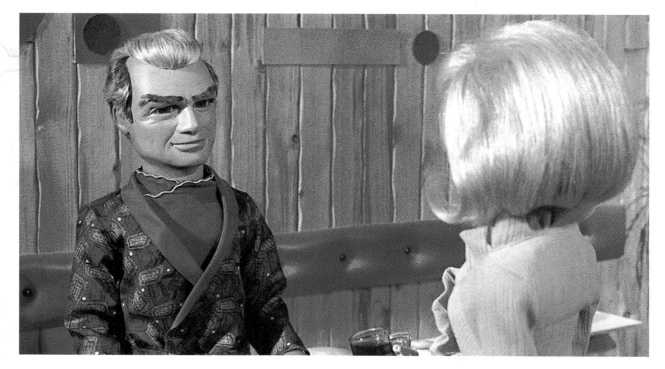

ABOVE AND RIGHT *Jeff Tracy enjoys a rare holiday at Lady Penelope's sheep farm in Bonga Bonga* (Atlantic Inferno).

SCOTT TRACY

The eldest of Jeff Tracy's sons, Scott was born on 4 April 2039 and is now twenty-six years old. Named after the pioneer astronaut Scott Malcolm Carpenter and educated at Yale and Oxford Universities, Scott was decorated for valour during his service with the US Air Force, before joining International Rescue.

As the pilot of Thunderbird 1, Scott is always the first to arrive at the danger zone, where he assesses the situation and quickly determines which special rescue equipment will be required for the task at hand. His complete lack of arrogance enables him to assist his brothers in even the most menial of tasks. In addition to his Thunderbird 1 duties, Scott often co-pilots Thunderbird 3 with his brother Alan, and has even been known to take occasional spells of duty aboard Thunderbird 5. Whenever his father, Jeff, is absent, Scott's seniority places him in command of the island headquarters.

Fast-talking and quick-thinking, with brains, brawn, daring and drive, Scott has the confidence to make instant decisions, backed by a fierce determination and unfaltering bravery.

BELOW *Scott pilots Thunderbird 1 on another rescue mission.*

BELOW LEFT *Scott at the controls of Thunderbird 1, with automatic camera detector behind.*

BELOW RIGHT *Scott co-pilots Thunderbird 3 (Ricochet).*

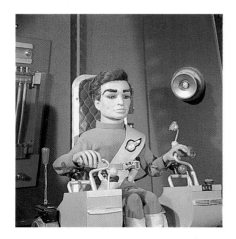

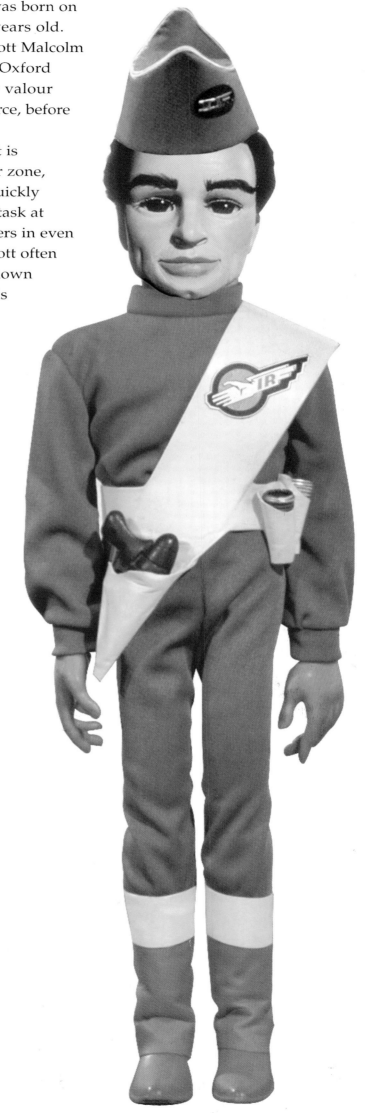

VIRGIL TRACY

The most serious of the Tracy brothers, Virgil was born on 15 August 2041 and is now twenty-four years old. Named after astronaut Virgil Grissom, he is an accomplished graduate of the Denver School of Advanced Technology. This gives him the experience and mechanical dexterity necessary to make him the ideal pilot of Thunderbird 2 and its various complex auxiliary rescue vehicles.

Like his brothers, Virgil never places technology above human needs, even if it means placing his own life in danger. As a result, he is always on hand, taking part in virtually every daring situation in which International Rescue is involved. Possessing a demeanour and maturity well beyond his years, Virgil is a complex young man who combines a physical strength and fearless bravery with a gentler side as a gifted artist and pianist.

BELOW *At the controls of the Master Elevator Car (*Trapped in the Sky*).*

BELOW *Virgil and Brains prepare to intercept the KLA pirate television satellite (*Ricochet*).*

ALAN TRACY

Named after astronaut Alan B. Shephard, Alan Tracy was born on 12 March 2044 and is now twenty-one years old. Caring and deeply romantic, he has a love of motor-racing and was a champion racing-car driver prior to becoming the pilot of Thunderbird 3. The blond-haired, baby-faced astronaut is utterly dedicated to International Rescue, meeting his great responsibilities with a maturity that belies his years. Yet there are times when his father still sees him as the college student whose rocket experiments went haywire, and accordingly treats him as a wayward schoolboy.

Educated at Colorado University, Alan is a great sportsman and practical joker. However, he is not without his quiet side and likes nothing better than to explore the rocks and potholes located in the more inaccessible points of Tracy Island. Apart from piloting Thunderbird 3, Alan also assists his brother John by taking turns at manning the space station, Thunderbird 5. He jealously guards his romantic relationship with Tin-Tin Kyrano, although he secretly harbours a passion for London agent Lady Penelope Creighton-Ward.

LEFT *Alan leaves Thunderbird 3 to rescue O'Shea and Loman (*Ricochet*).*

BELOW *Alan flies Thunderbird 1 to the danger zone (*Atlantic Inferno*).*

GORDON TRACY

Born on 14 February 2043, Gordon Tracy is a twenty-two-year-old who revels in all aquatic sports, from skin-diving to water-skiing. Named after astronaut Leroy Gordon Cooper, he is a highly trained aquanaut, with stints in the Submarine Service and the World Aquanaut Security Patrol under his belt. During his time with the WASPs, Gordon commanded a deep-sea bathyscaphe and spent a year beneath the ocean investigating marine farming methods. An expert oceanographer, he is also the designer of a unique underwater breathing apparatus, which he has modified and improved for International Rescue.

Shortly before International Rescue began operating, Gordon was involved in a hydrofoil speedboat crash when his vessel capsized at 400 knots. The craft was completely shattered and Gordon spent four months in a hospital bed. Now, as the pilot of Thunderbird 4, he commands the world's most advanced and versatile one-man submarine. Good-natured and high-spirited, he possesses a strength and tenacity that make him a respected leader and commander. He is also one of the world's fastest freestyle swimmers and is a past Olympic champion at the butterfly stroke.

RIGHT *Gordon at the controls of Thunderbird 4.*

RIGHT *Gordon searches for Ned Cook and his cameraman (Terror in New York City).*

JOHN TRACY

Born on 8 October 2040, twenty-five-year-old John Tracy was educated at Harvard and followed in his father's footsteps to become an astronaut prior to his involvement with International Rescue. Named after astronaut John Glenn, he is an electronics expert with a degree in laser communication. John is the quietest and most intellectual of the Tracy brothers, slighter in build than his siblings and tremendously lithe and graceful.

As space monitor for International Rescue stationed aboard Thunderbird 5, John has ample time on his hands to indulge his favourite pastime, astronomy. Four astronomy and outer space textbooks have been published bearing his name, and his incessant space searching led to the discovery of the Tracy quasar system. His duties aboard Thunderbird 5 nonetheless leave him feeling frustrated that he is unable to take part in as many rescue missions as his siblings.

LEFT *John responds to a distress call from Seascape (Atlantic Inferno).*

LEFT *John relaxes by the pool (Danger at Ocean Deep).*

BELOW *John intercepts a message from Fireflash (Trapped in the Sky).*

BRAINS

Born on 14 November 2040, Brains was orphaned when a hurricane struck his Michigan home. He was adopted at the age of twelve by a Cambridge University professor who recognized the boy's genius and encouraged his phenomenal learning abilities. During a worldwide search for a brilliant scientist who could help him accomplish his plans for International Rescue, Jeff Tracy discovered Brains nervously delivering a lecture at a cultural hall in Paris. Brains recognized in Jeff Tracy a philanthropic entrepreneur striving to save mankind and accepted his challenge without hesitation.

As the inventor of all of International Rescue's dazzling machines, Brains is an esteemed and valuable part of the secret organization. An incurable perfectionist, the twenty-five-year-old is never satisfied with his creations and is often to be found endlessly modifying and tinkering with his machines. His idea of off-duty relaxation includes studying trigonometry and thermodynamics, while designing new ways of improving Braman, a robot that he hopes will one day defeat him at chess.

To protect his identity in the outside world while developing incredible new machines and aircraft for business and industry (such as Skythrust and Skyship One), Brains goes by the alias of Hiram K. Hackenbacker. His real name is unknown.

LADY PENELOPE CREIGHTON-WARD

Born on 24 December 2039, Lady Penelope Creighton-Ward is the twenty-six-year-old daughter of aristocrat Sir Hugh Creighton-Ward and his wife, Amelia. Lady Penelope inherited her father's spirit and determination, craving danger, action and intrigue, so after completing her education at Rowden and a finishing school in Switzerland, she rejected the aristocracy's endless round of social engagements and became a secret agent. It was while working as the chief operative of the Federal Agents Bureau that Lady Penelope first met Jeff Tracy, and she immediately accepted his invitation to become International Rescue's London agent, a key part of the organization's network of undercover agents.

Stylish and fashionable in every aspect of her life, Lady Penelope owns FAB 1, an incredible six-wheeled Rolls-Royce, as well as Seabird, a 40-foot ocean-going cruiser, FAB 2, a sleek private yacht, and FAB 3, a prize-winning racehorse. Her clothes are specially created for her by top fashion designers Elaine Wickfen and François Lemaire, and she wears an exclusive perfume, Soupçon de Péril, mixed for her in Paris by Jacques Verre.

Working from Creighton-Ward Mansion, her eighteenth-century stately home at Foxleyheath in southern England, Lady Penelope appears to those ignorant of her secret life to be just another member of the English landed gentry. But with her poise and nerves of steel, she has proved time and again to be an invaluable addition to the International Rescue team.

ALOYSIUS PARKER

Born on 30 May, 2013, Aloysius Parker is the last of a long line of faithful Cockney retainers who have served the English aristocracy for centuries. However, unable to find employment as a butler, he fell in with various villains in the London underworld who taught him the tricks of the trade. Known to his new friends as 'Nosey', Parker soon gained a reputation for himself as one of the world's finest safe-crackers and cat burglars, a reputation that also landed him in Parkmoor Scrubs prison for a spell.

After his release, he attempted to make an honest living, but he soon fell back into his old ways and was caught by Lady Penelope Creighton-Ward while he was helping himself to the contents of an oil tycoon's safe. Penelope had heard of Parker's superior talents and offered him a working partnership in her espionage activities, employing him as both butler at Creighton-Ward Mansion and chauffeur of her Rolls-Royce, FAB 1.

KYRANO

The son of a Malayan plantation owner, Kyrano turned his back on material gain after his inheritance was usurped by his evil half-brother, the Hood. Becoming an expert botanist, he spent a number of years at Kew Gardens, before being invited to Kennedy Space Center to help develop synthetic food from plants. It was here that Kyrano first met Jeff Tracy.

Later, Kyrano became head chef at the Paris Hilton, but he was happy to abandon this position when he was contacted by Jeff Tracy to help with the Tracy Island domestic arrangements.

A vital part of the smooth running of the secret island base, Kyrano has only one failing: his susceptibility to the evil influence of his half-brother, who often uses Kyrano as a pawn. Kyrano's exact age is unknown as his birth certificate was lost in Malaya.

TIN-TIN KYRANO

Born on 20 June 2043, Tin-Tin Kyrano is the daughter of the Tracys' faithful family retainer, and the unlikely half-niece of their arch-enemy the Hood. Her education in America and Europe was paid for by Jeff Tracy as a token of his gratitude for her father's loyal services, and she graduated with degrees in higher mathematics, advanced technical theory and engineering. She joined International Rescue directly after completing her education, assisting Brains and organizing the maintenance of all of the Thunderbirds vehicles.

Also a qualified pilot, Tin-Tin's main interests outside her work include pop music, water-skiing, swimming and designing her own clothes. She enjoys a playful relationship with Alan, whom she adores. Her name comes from the Malaysian word for 'sweet'.

THE HOOD

Feared as the world's foremost villain, the Hood (so named because of his many disguises) is the half-brother of Kyrano and wields an uncanny, supernatural power over him. Unlike his brother, the Hood is massive in stature and his main aim in life is the acquisition of wealth regardless of justice and ethics. His primary target is International Rescue, as the plans of their incredible vehicles and machines could make him rich beyond his wildest imaginings.

Operating from a strange temple hidden deep in the Malaysian jungle, the Hood has successfully eluded capture by the world's security forces for a great many years. Ruthless and calculating beyond comprehension, he uses mystical powers, steeped in voodoo and black magic, to deadly effect, allowing nothing to stand in the way of his evil objectives.

His criminal record indicates that he was born on 17 July 2018.

TRACY ISLAND

TRACY FAMILY HOME AND SECRET INTERNATIONAL RESCUE BASE

To the outside world, Tracy Island is the luxury home of multi-millionaire Jeff Tracy. An ex-astronaut and the founder of a number of successful international engineering and aerospace companies, he lives here with his mother and five sons. Also resident on Tracy Island are the housekeeper, Kyrano, his daughter, Tin-Tin, and Brains, a scientific genius. Behind the domestic façade, the island is in fact the secret base of International Rescue.

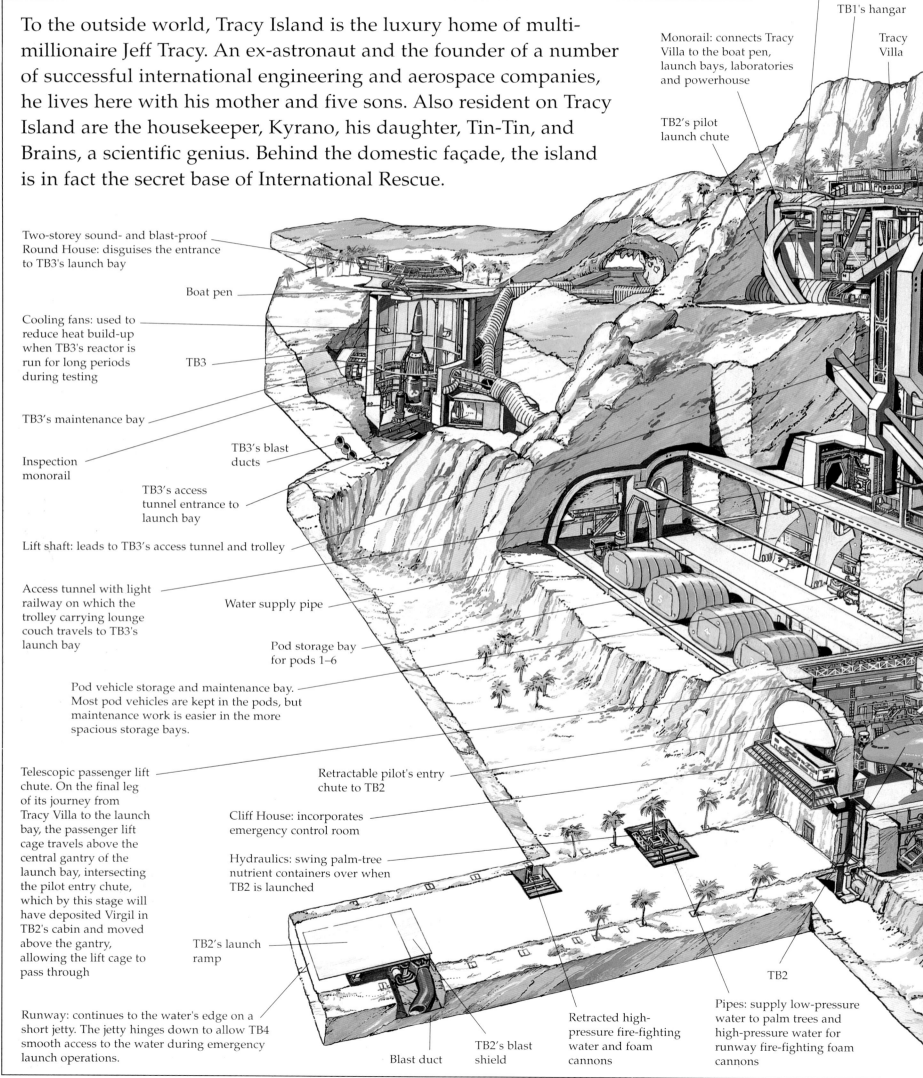

Turntable: enables Virgil to approach TB2's cabin via the launch chute feet first

TB1's hangar

Tracy Villa

Monorail: connects Tracy Villa to the boat pen, launch bays, laboratories and powerhouse

TB2's pilot launch chute

Two-storey sound- and blast-proof Round House: disguises the entrance to TB3's launch bay

Boat pen

Cooling fans: used to reduce heat build-up when TB3's reactor is run for long periods during testing

TB3

TB3's maintenance bay

Inspection monorail

TB3's blast ducts

TB3's access tunnel entrance to launch bay

Lift shaft: leads to TB3's access tunnel and trolley

Access tunnel with light railway on which the trolley carrying lounge couch travels to TB3's launch bay

Water supply pipe

Pod storage bay for pods 1–6

Pod vehicle storage and maintenance bay. Most pod vehicles are kept in the pods, but maintenance work is easier in the more spacious storage bays.

Telescopic passenger lift chute. On the final leg of its journey from Tracy Villa to the launch bay, the passenger lift cage travels above the central gantry of the launch bay, intersecting the pilot entry chute, which by this stage will have deposited Virgil in TB2's cabin and moved above the gantry, allowing the lift cage to pass through

Retractable pilot's entry chute to TB2

Cliff House: incorporates emergency control room

Hydraulics: swing palm-tree nutrient containers over when TB2 is launched

TB2's launch ramp

Runway: continues to the water's edge on a short jetty. The jetty hinges down to allow TB4 smooth access to the water during emergency launch operations.

Blast duct

TB2's blast shield

Retracted high-pressure fire-fighting water and foam cannons

TB2

Pipes: supply low-pressure water to palm trees and high-pressure water for runway fire-fighting foam cannons

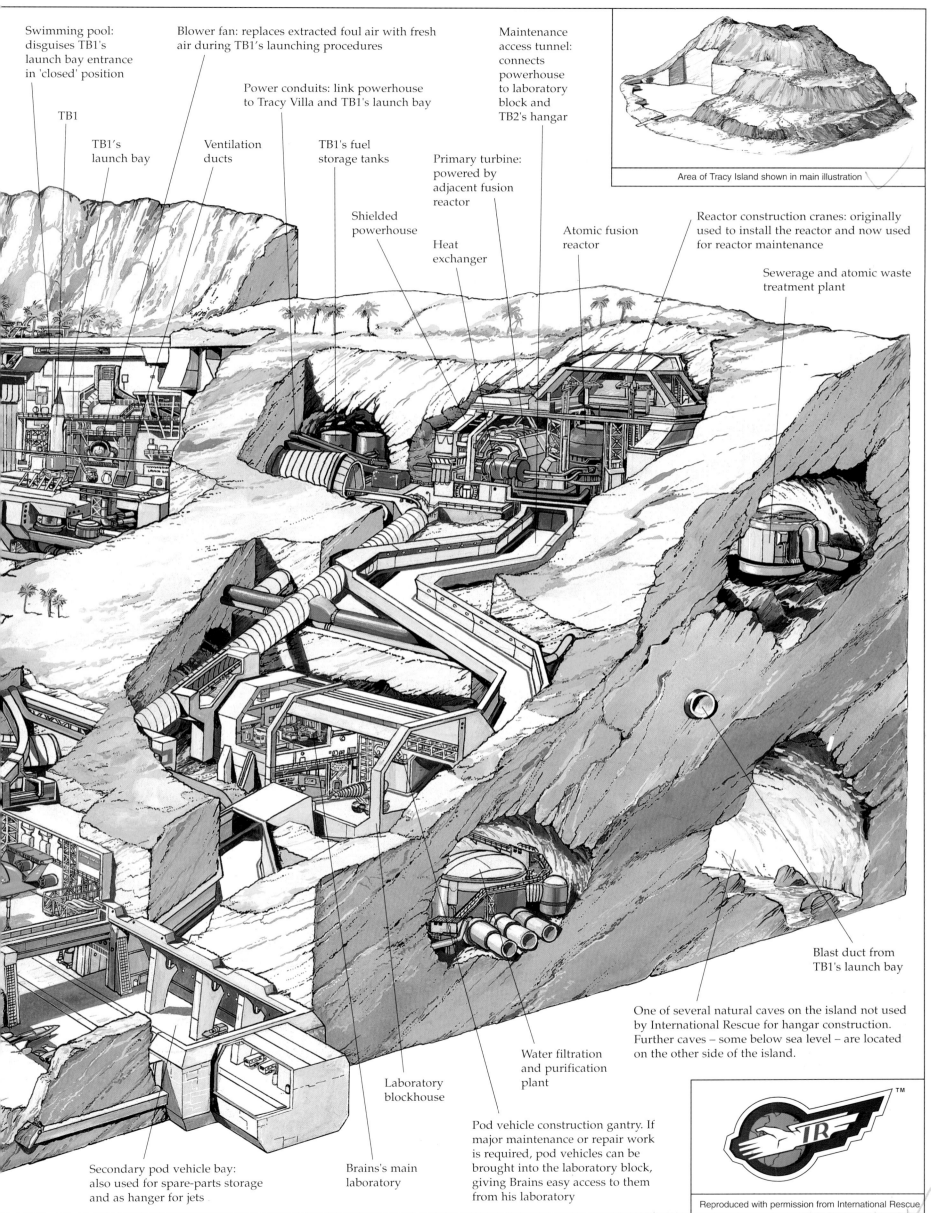

Swimming pool: disguises TB1's launch bay entrance in 'closed' position

TB1

TB1's launch bay

Ventilation ducts

Blower fan: replaces extracted foul air with fresh air during TB1's launching procedures

Power conduits: link powerhouse to Tracy Villa and TB1's launch bay

TB1's fuel storage tanks

Shielded powerhouse

Heat exchanger

Primary turbine: powered by adjacent fusion reactor

Maintenance access tunnel: connects powerhouse to laboratory block and TB2's hangar

Atomic fusion reactor

Reactor construction cranes: originally used to install the reactor and now used for reactor maintenance

Sewerage and atomic waste treatment plant

Area of Tracy Island shown in main illustration

Blast duct from TB1's launch bay

One of several natural caves on the island not used by International Rescue for hangar construction. Further caves – some below sea level – are located on the other side of the island.

Water filtration and purification plant

Laboratory blockhouse

Pod vehicle construction gantry. If major maintenance or repair work is required, pod vehicles can be brought into the laboratory block, giving Brains easy access to them from his laboratory

Secondary pod vehicle bay: also used for spare-parts storage and as hanger for jets

Brains's main laboratory

21

THUNDERBIRD 1

INTERNATIONAL RESCUE'S HIGH-SPEED RECONNAISSANCE CRAFT

Designed to reach disaster zones quickly, Thunderbird 1 can travel at 15,000 m.p.h. This allows pilot Scott Tracy to assess the situation and report back to Tracy Island or Thunderbird 2 with details of how best to proceed with the rescue. Although TB2 carries the majority of the rescue equipment for any given mission, TB1 is equipped with heat-sensing systems, a remote hover camera, sonar equipment and a mobile control unit, from which Scott can direct rescue operations.

TECHNICAL DATA

LENGTH: .... 115 feet
WINGSPAN: .... 80 feet
DIAMETER: .... 12 feet
WEIGHT: .... 140 tons
MAXIMUM SPEED: ...... 15,000 m.p.h.
MAXIMUM ALTITUDE ATTAINED:
.... 150,000 feet
RANGE: .... unlimited
POWER SOURCE: .... atomic fusion reactor
ENGINES:
    4 variable-cycle gas turbine engines
    4 booster rockets
    1 variable-mode engine operating as a
       high-performance sustainer rocket
       for launch or boost or as a variable-
       cycle gas turbine engine in flight
    1 vertical take-off variable-mode engine
       operating as a rocket or variable-
       cycle gas turbine hover jet
    Pitch and yaw jets: 20 forward and
       25 rear
PILOT: .... Scott Tracy

Remote-controlled hover camera: uses anti-gravity technology to allow Scott to view the disaster area from the safety of Thunderbird 1's cabin, needed if there are poisonous gases or unstable ground. Also incorporated is a body-heat detection system to find victims buried underground or in earthquake rubble.

Fuselage refrigeration unit

Auxiliary motors and batteries

Life-support systems and atmosphere-recycling unit

Control console computer interface: transfers piloting commands from ergonomically simplified control console to flight computer

Air-recycling duct

Computerized instrumentation system: uses 'nano' technology to allow simplified control of aircraft at high speed

Forward pitch and yaw jets

Starboard window hatch

Forward radar and body-heat detection systems

Wing carry-through box containing wing hinge with adjacent hydraulic ram controlling wing angle

Vertical take-off fuel tanks

Variable-mode vertical take-off rocket and hover jet

Heat-resistant cahelium-bonded nose cone

Retracted machine cannon

Pilot exit hatch

Folding ladder: moves forward and unfolds telescopically downwards to allow access via underside exit hatch to pilot's cabin

Oxygen tanks

Pressure bulkhead

Sonar tracking system: sonar can be lowered into water from the underside of TB1 while in hover mode and is used to register life-signs and measure underwater depths and distances. It is often used in location-finding with Thunderbird 4.

Pilot's seat: rotates to remain upright when TB1 changes from vertical to horizontal flight

Bulkhead supporting pilot's seat

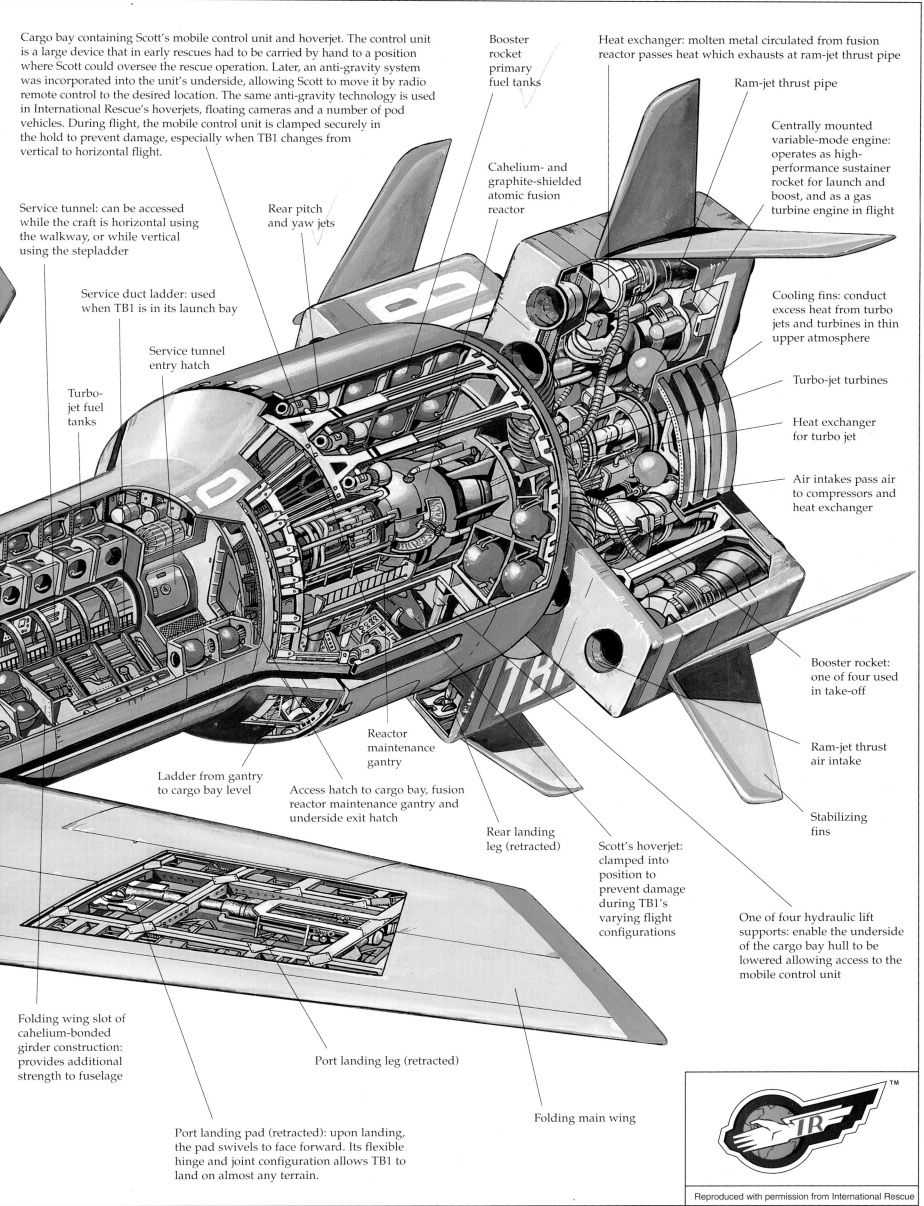

Cargo bay containing Scott's mobile control unit and hoverjet. The control unit is a large device that in early rescues had to be carried by hand to a position where Scott could oversee the rescue operation. Later, an anti-gravity system was incorporated into the unit's underside, allowing Scott to move it by radio remote control to the desired location. The same anti-gravity technology is used in International Rescue's hoverjets, floating cameras and a number of pod vehicles. During flight, the mobile control unit is clamped securely in the hold to prevent damage, especially when TB1 changes from vertical to horizontal flight.

Booster rocket primary fuel tanks

Heat exchanger: molten metal circulated from fusion reactor passes heat which exhausts at ram-jet thrust pipe

Ram-jet thrust pipe

Centrally mounted variable-mode engine: operates as high-performance sustainer rocket for launch and boost, and as a gas turbine engine in flight

Cahelium- and graphite-shielded atomic fusion reactor

Service tunnel: can be accessed while the craft is horizontal using the walkway, or while vertical using the stepladder

Rear pitch and yaw jets

Cooling fins: conduct excess heat from turbo jets and turbines in thin upper atmosphere

Service duct ladder: used when TB1 is in its launch bay

Turbo-jet turbines

Service tunnel entry hatch

Heat exchanger for turbo jet

Turbo-jet fuel tanks

Air intakes pass air to compressors and heat exchanger

Booster rocket: one of four used in take-off

Reactor maintenance gantry

Ram-jet thrust air intake

Ladder from gantry to cargo bay level

Access hatch to cargo bay, fusion reactor maintenance gantry and underside exit hatch

Rear landing leg (retracted)

Stabilizing fins

Scott's hoverjet: clamped into position to prevent damage during TB1's varying flight configurations

One of four hydraulic lift supports: enable the underside of the cargo bay hull to be lowered allowing access to the mobile control unit

Folding wing slot of cahelium-bonded girder construction: provides additional strength to fuselage

Port landing leg (retracted)

Folding main wing

Port landing pad (retracted): upon landing, the pad swivels to face forward. Its flexible hinge and joint configuration allows TB1 to land on almost any terrain.

Renowned for its power and strength, Thunderbird 2 is constructed of an alloy developed by Brains which incorporates a heat-resistant and extremely strong metal discovered in the early twenty-first century called cahelium. With six interchangeable pods, TB2 carries vital heavy engineering and life-saving equipment to the danger zone at a speed of up to 5,000 m.p.h. and can achieve a maximum altitude of 100,000 feet.

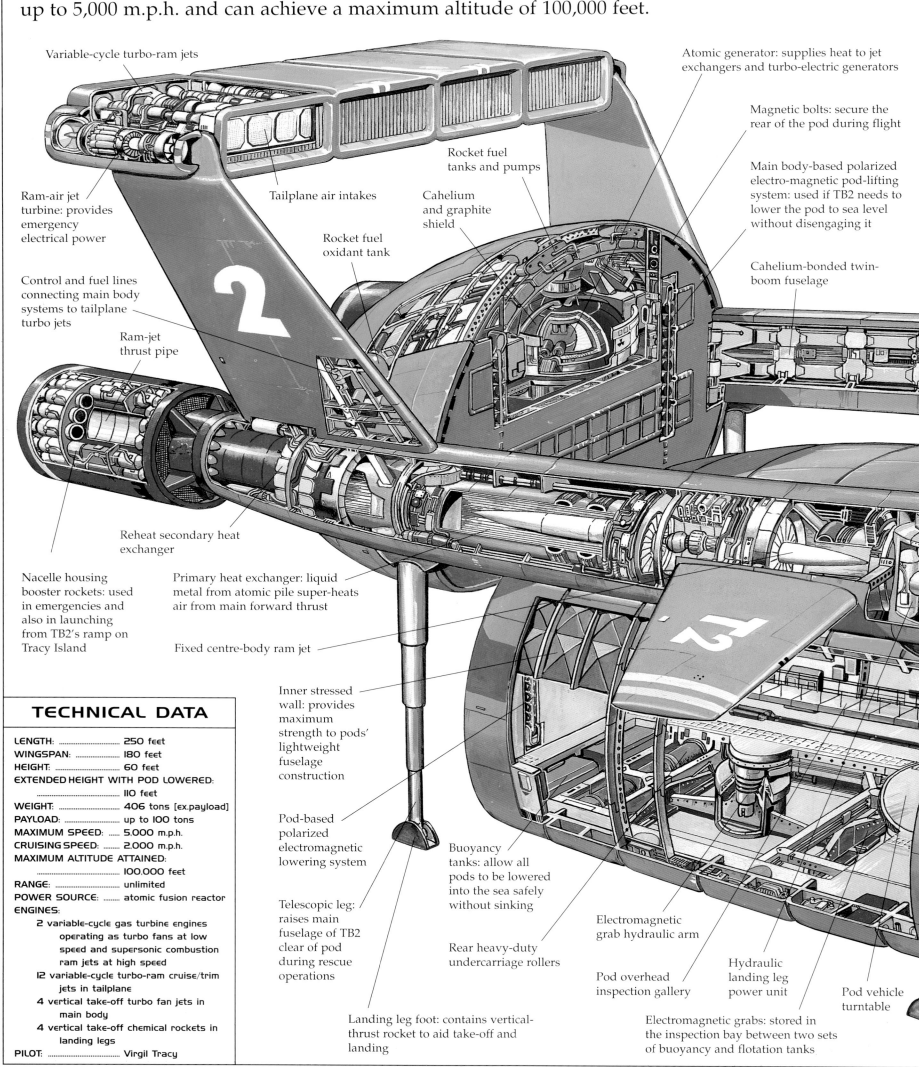

Variable-cycle turbo-ram jets

Ram-air jet turbine: provides emergency electrical power

Control and fuel lines connecting main body systems to tailplane turbo jets

Ram-jet thrust pipe

Reheat secondary heat exchanger

Nacelle housing booster rockets: used in emergencies and also in launching from TB2's ramp on Tracy Island

Primary heat exchanger: liquid metal from atomic pile super-heats air from main forward thrust

Fixed centre-body ram jet

Tailplane air intakes

Rocket fuel tanks and pumps

Cahelium and graphite shield

Rocket fuel oxidant tank

Atomic generator: supplies heat to jet exchangers and turbo-electric generators

Magnetic bolts: secure the rear of the pod during flight

Main body-based polarized electro-magnetic pod-lifting system: used if TB2 needs to lower the pod to sea level without disengaging it

Cahelium-bonded twin-boom fuselage

Inner stressed wall: provides maximum strength to pods' lightweight fuselage construction

Pod-based polarized electromagnetic lowering system

Telescopic leg: raises main fuselage of TB2 clear of pod during rescue operations

Buoyancy tanks: allow all pods to be lowered into the sea safely without sinking

Rear heavy-duty undercarriage rollers

Electromagnetic grab hydraulic arm

Pod overhead inspection gallery

Hydraulic landing leg power unit

Pod vehicle turntable

Landing leg foot: contains vertical-thrust rocket to aid take-off and landing

Electromagnetic grabs: stored in the inspection bay between two sets of buoyancy and flotation tanks

TECHNICAL DATA

LENGTH: .... 250 feet
WINGSPAN: .... 180 feet
HEIGHT: .... 60 feet
EXTENDED HEIGHT WITH POD LOWERED:
.... 110 feet
WEIGHT: .... 406 tons [ex.payload]
PAYLOAD: .... up to 100 tons
MAXIMUM SPEED: ...... 5,000 m.p.h.
CRUISING SPEED: ...... 2,000 m.p.h.
MAXIMUM ALTITUDE ATTAINED:
.... 100,000 feet
RANGE: .... unlimited
POWER SOURCE: .... atomic fusion reactor
ENGINES:
    2 variable-cycle gas turbine engines
       operating as turbo fans at low
       speed and supersonic combustion
       ram jets at high speed
    12 variable-cycle turbo-ram cruise/trim
       jets in tailplane
    4 vertical take-off turbo fan jets in
       main body
    4 vertical take-off chemical rockets in
       landing legs
PILOT: .... Virgil Tracy

THUNDERBIRD 2

INTERNATIONAL RESCUE'S HEAVY-DUTY EQUIPMENT TRANSPORTER

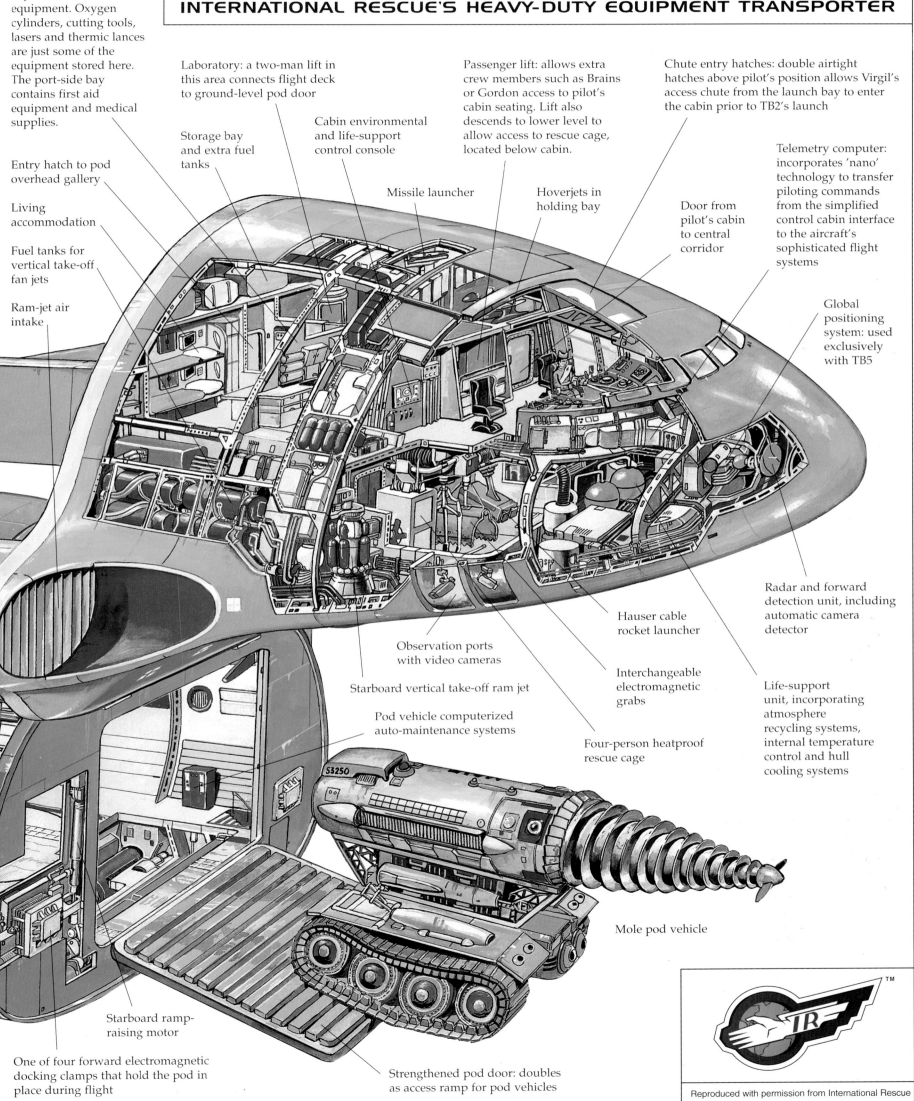

Starboard storage bay: holds rescue equipment. Oxygen cylinders, cutting tools, lasers and thermic lances are just some of the equipment stored here. The port-side bay contains first aid equipment and medical supplies.

Entry hatch to pod overhead gallery

Living accommodation

Fuel tanks for vertical take-off fan jets

Ram-jet air intake

Laboratory: a two-man lift in this area connects flight deck to ground-level pod door

Storage bay and extra fuel tanks

Cabin environmental and life-support control console

Missile launcher

Passenger lift: allows extra crew members such as Brains or Gordon access to pilot's cabin seating. Lift also descends to lower level to allow access to rescue cage, located below cabin.

Hoverjets in holding bay

Chute entry hatches: double airtight hatches above pilot's position allows Virgil's access chute from the launch bay to enter the cabin prior to TB2's launch

Door from pilot's cabin to central corridor

Telemetry computer: incorporates 'nano' technology to transfer piloting commands from the simplified control cabin interface to the aircraft's sophisticated flight systems

Global positioning system: used exclusively with TB5

Radar and forward detection unit, including automatic camera detector

Hauser cable rocket launcher

Interchangeable electromagnetic grabs

Life-support unit, incorporating atmosphere recycling systems, internal temperature control and hull cooling systems

Observation ports with video cameras

Starboard vertical take-off ram jet

Pod vehicle computerized auto-maintenance systems

Four-person heatproof rescue cage

Mole pod vehicle

Starboard ramp-raising motor

One of four forward electromagnetic docking clamps that hold the pod in place during flight

Strengthened pod door: doubles as access ramp for pod vehicles

Transported in Thunderbird 2, the pod vehicles play an essential part in rescue operations. Although there is a storage and service bay on Tracy Island, they tend to be kept on stand-by in TB2's six pods to save time. Most vehicles are designed for specific situations, such as the Mole for burrowing and Thunderbird 4 for underwater work. However, a number of them were purchased by International Rescue and adapted. These include a fire tender and two heavy-duty general-purpose trucks which have been upgraded for use as a mobile transmitter and an extra fire appliance.

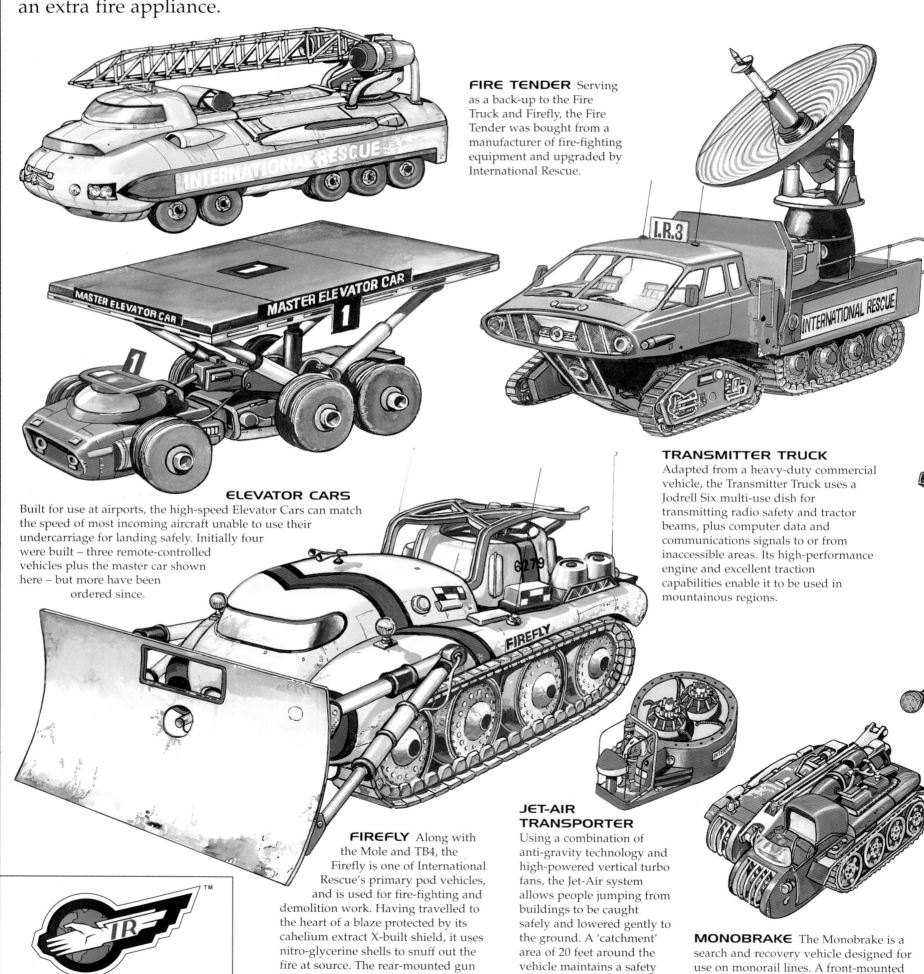

FIRE TENDER Serving as a back-up to the Fire Truck and Firefly, the Fire Tender was bought from a manufacturer of fire-fighting equipment and upgraded by International Rescue.

ELEVATOR CARS
Built for use at airports, the high-speed Elevator Cars can match the speed of most incoming aircraft unable to use their undercarriage for landing safely. Initially four were built – three remote-controlled vehicles plus the master car shown here – but more have been ordered since.

TRANSMITTER TRUCK
Adapted from a heavy-duty commercial vehicle, the Transmitter Truck uses a Jodrell Six multi-use dish for transmitting radio safety and tractor beams, plus computer data and communications signals to or from inaccessible areas. Its high-performance engine and excellent traction capabilities enable it to be used in mountainous regions.

FIREFLY Along with the Mole and TB4, the Firefly is one of International Rescue's primary pod vehicles, and is used for fire-fighting and demolition work. Having travelled to the heart of a blaze protected by its cahelium extract X-built shield, it uses nitro-glycerine shells to snuff out the fire at source. The rear-mounted gun can also extinguish fires using water or foam.

JET-AIR TRANSPORTER
Using a combination of anti-gravity technology and high-powered vertical turbo fans, the Jet-Air system allows people jumping from buildings to be caught safely and lowered gently to the ground. A 'catchment' area of 20 feet around the vehicle maintains a safety margin when people are jumping.

MONOBRAKE The Monobrake is a search and recovery vehicle designed for use on monorail lines. A front-mounted telescopic arm can be attached to the overhead monorail for greater speed.

MOBILE CRANE
A vehicle used primarily to lift rescue personnel up to 100 feet in order to reach tall buildings, trees, transmitter masts and even moving vehicles such as the Crablogger

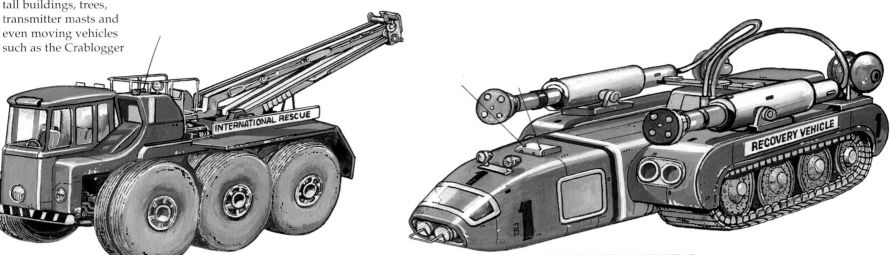

RECOVERY VEHICLE
The Recovery Vehicles are used to haul great weights – such as aircraft or trains – out of pits, lakes and rivers.

NEUTRALIZER TRACTOR A small mobile device for disabling the electronics and radio control systems of explosive devices, the Neutralizer can also disrupt computer systems by overriding incoming data signals transmitted by carrier waves from external sources.

THUNDERIZER To assist those trapped in tall buildings, the Thunderizer can fire steel-cylinder rescue packs with computer-controlled precision to upper-floor windows. The cylinders contain a variety of equipment, from anti-gravity jet packs to oxygen tanks and hand-held fire-fighting tools. Explosive projectiles can also be launched if appropriate.

EXCAVATOR Sometimes used in conjunction with the Mole and Domo, the Excavator is a high-powered rock-crushing machine for clearing rough ground, and is particularly useful in areas affected by landslides.

LASER CUTTER VEHICLE If access to a vault or bunker is required, the laser cutter is used to gain precise and rapid entry to the premises. The laser gun has a number of variable cutting options, from single beams to pulsed energy bursts.

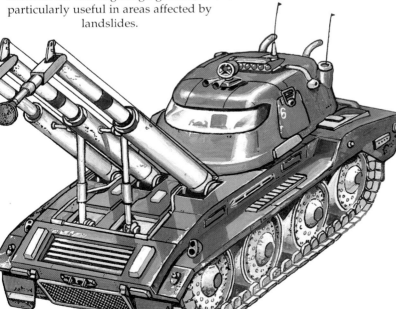

FIRE TRUCK
Like the Transmitter Truck, this is a commercial vehicle which has been purchased and adapted for International Rescue's use. It can fire nitro-glycerine shells to neutralize blazes as well as pumping water and foam onto fires.

DOMO The Demolition and Object Moving Operator uses artificial-gravity fields within its three suction pods to stabilize walls or lift objects weighing up to 50 tons. It is used to clear the disaster zone of heavy objects or secure dangerous buildings prior to the use of other vehicles such as the Mole.

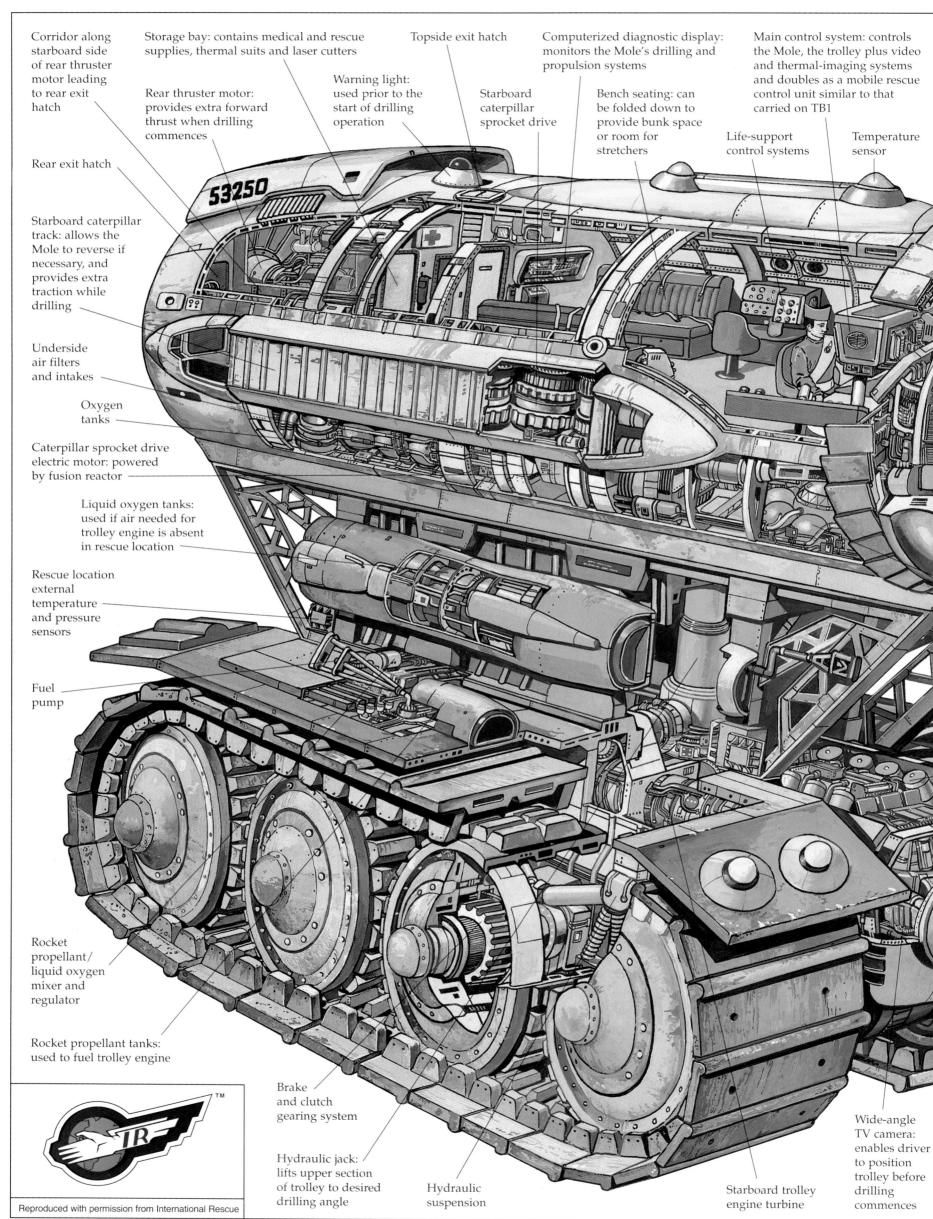

Corridor along starboard side of rear thruster motor leading to rear exit hatch

Storage bay: contains medical and rescue supplies, thermal suits and laser cutters

Topside exit hatch

Computerized diagnostic display: monitors the Mole's drilling and propulsion systems

Main control system: controls the Mole, the trolley plus video and thermal-imaging systems and doubles as a mobile rescue control unit similar to that carried on TB1

Rear thruster motor: provides extra forward thrust when drilling commences

Warning light: used prior to the start of drilling operation

Starboard caterpillar sprocket drive

Bench seating: can be folded down to provide bunk space or room for stretchers

Life-support control systems

Temperature sensor

Rear exit hatch

Starboard caterpillar track: allows the Mole to reverse if necessary, and provides extra traction while drilling

Underside air filters and intakes

Oxygen tanks

Caterpillar sprocket drive electric motor: powered by fusion reactor

Liquid oxygen tanks: used if air needed for trolley engine is absent in rescue location

Rescue location external temperature and pressure sensors

Fuel pump

Rocket propellant/ liquid oxygen mixer and regulator

Rocket propellant tanks: used to fuel trolley engine

Brake and clutch gearing system

Hydraulic jack: lifts upper section of trolley to desired drilling angle

Hydraulic suspension

Starboard trolley engine turbine

Wide-angle TV camera: enables driver to position trolley before drilling commences

53250

28

THE MOLE

INTERNATIONAL RESCUE'S DRILLING AND BURROWING MACHINE

Main computer: handles all functions so that driver can concentrate on the mission using simplified control systems on the cabin

Shielded nuclear fusion reactor: provides power for electric generators to operate the drill, caterpillar tracks and rear thruster

Electric generator

Electric motor powered by reactor: drives sprocket rings via multiple gearing system

Multiple bearing system within drive sprocket ring: turns drill bit

Drill bit, constructed from Formula C30/1, a cahelium-derived alloy that can cut through virtually all known metals

Acoustic detector and 3D thermal-imaging system: scans the ground ahead of the Mole to detect buried victims. Positions of victims can be logged on the Mole's computer and the data transferred to TB2. More delicate rescue operations can then commence, using smaller drilling equipment and hand-held laser cutters.

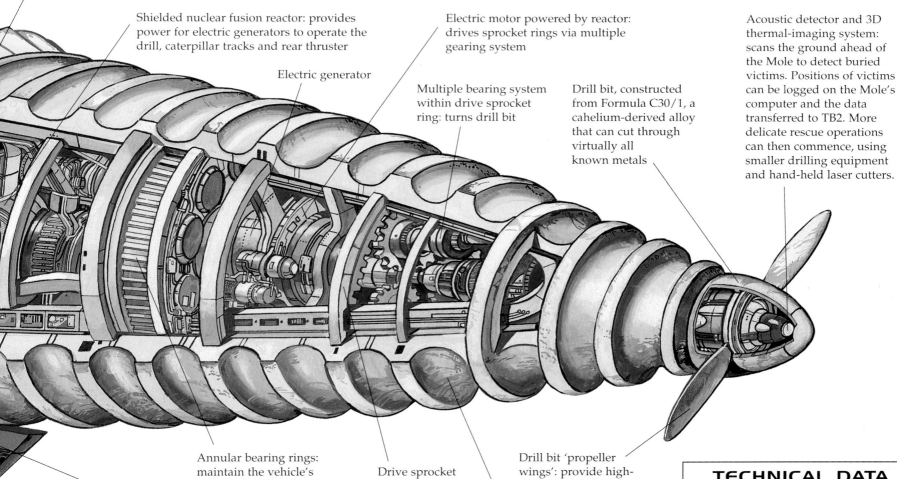

Air recycling plant and life-support system

Trolley

Annular bearing rings: maintain the vehicle's structural integrity as the drill rotates at high speed

Drive sprocket ring

Drill bit 'propeller wings': provide high-speed cutting edge

1,000 b.h.p. high-compression engine: uses rocket propellant and air as fuel. The trolley is controlled from the driver's console in the Mole itself.

Forward warning and hazard lights

Main air intakes: provide oxidant to mix with rocket propellant for trolley's engine

Revolving outer drill casing, constructed from cahelium and Formula C30/1 additives. Tapered cone configuration allows the Mole to tunnel underground with reduced resistance.

Multiple missile launch system: used for demolition if no victims can be found using the thermal-imaging system in the Mole's drill bit

TECHNICAL DATA

MOLE SPECIFICATIONS
LENGTH:	60 feet
WIDTH:	12 feet
WEIGHT:	12 tons
MAXIMUM DRILLING SPEED:	15 m.p.h.
POWER:	Nuclear-fusion-powered electric motors

TROLLEY SPECIFICATIONS
LENGTH:	38 feet
WIDTH:	24 feet
WEIGHT:	18 tons
MAXIMUM SPEED:	50 m.p.h.
POWER:	1,000 b.h.p. high-compression dual-turbine engine

Carried to the rescue zone in Thunderbird 2, the Mole is one of the larger pod vehicles at 30 tons. It is used to help recover victims trapped in collapsed buildings or buried underground. Despite its size and tremendous power, the Mole can be operated with great precision so that buried victims are not endangered by rock falls started by the movement of the drill. This is thanks to the three-dimensional thermal-imaging system built into the drill bit. The Mole is carried to the rescue zone from its pod on a trolley and then tilted to a near-vertical position to commence drilling. Caterpillar tracks on each side enable the Mole to return to the surface, reversing back up on to the trolley on completion of a rescue.

THUNDERBIRD 3

INTERNATIONAL RESCUE'S SPACE RESCUE ROCKET

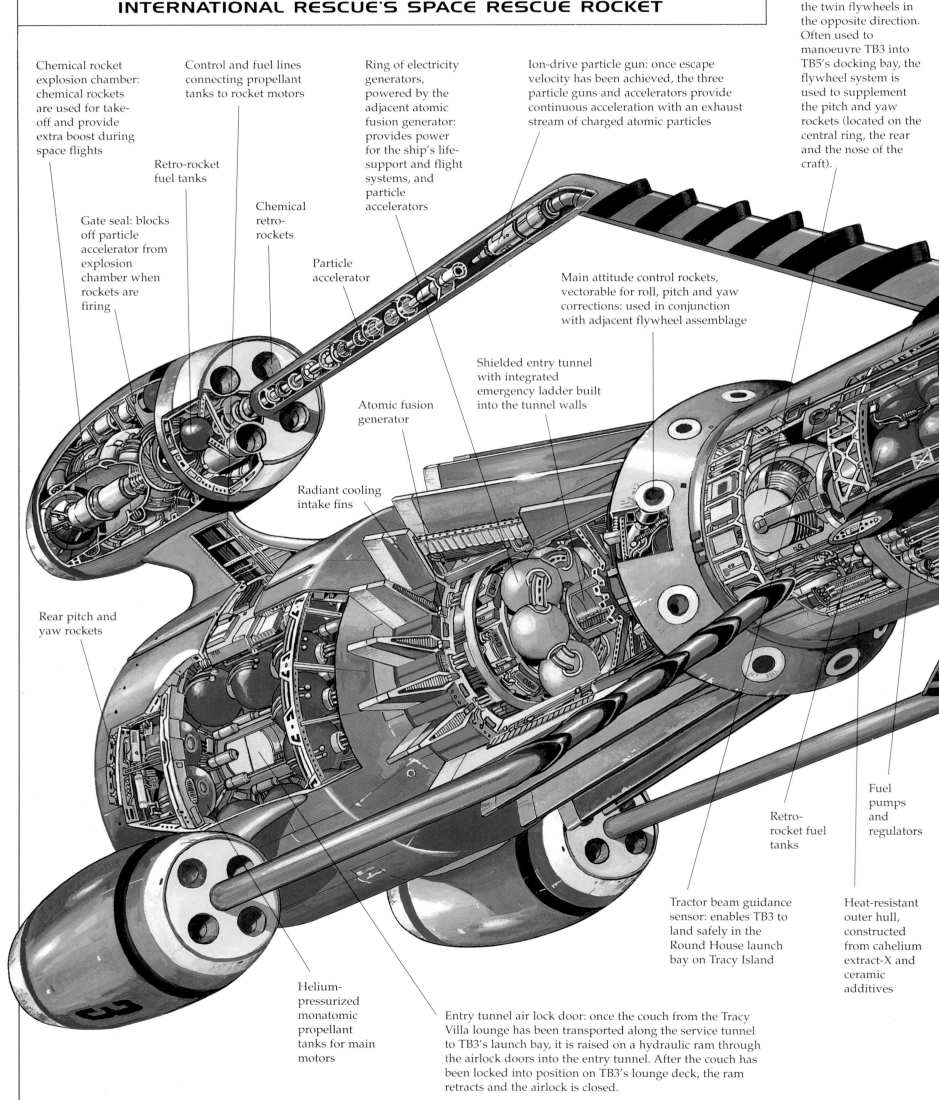

Dual flywheel motor assemblage: attitude alteration can be achieved by spinning the twin flywheels in the opposite direction. Often used to manoeuvre TB3 into TB5's docking bay, the flywheel system is used to supplement the pitch and yaw rockets (located on the central ring, the rear and the nose of the craft).

Chemical rocket explosion chamber: chemical rockets are used for take-off and provide extra boost during space flights

Control and fuel lines connecting propellant tanks to rocket motors

Ring of electricity generators, powered by the adjacent atomic fusion generator: provides power for the ship's life-support and flight systems, and particle accelerators

Ion-drive particle gun: once escape velocity has been achieved, the three particle guns and accelerators provide continuous acceleration with an exhaust stream of charged atomic particles

Retro-rocket fuel tanks

Gate seal: blocks off particle accelerator from explosion chamber when rockets are firing

Chemical retro-rockets

Particle accelerator

Main attitude control rockets, vectorable for roll, pitch and yaw corrections: used in conjunction with adjacent flywheel assemblage

Shielded entry tunnel with integrated emergency ladder built into the tunnel walls

Atomic fusion generator

Radiant cooling intake fins

Rear pitch and yaw rockets

Fuel pumps and regulators

Retro-rocket fuel tanks

Tractor beam guidance sensor: enables TB3 to land safely in the Round House launch bay on Tracy Island

Heat-resistant outer hull, constructed from cahelium extract-X and ceramic additives

Helium-pressurized monatomic propellant tanks for main motors

Entry tunnel air lock door: once the couch from the Tracy Villa lounge has been transported along the service tunnel to TB3's launch bay, it is raised on a hydraulic ram through the airlock doors into the entry tunnel. After the couch has been locked into position on TB3's lounge deck, the ram retracts and the airlock is closed.

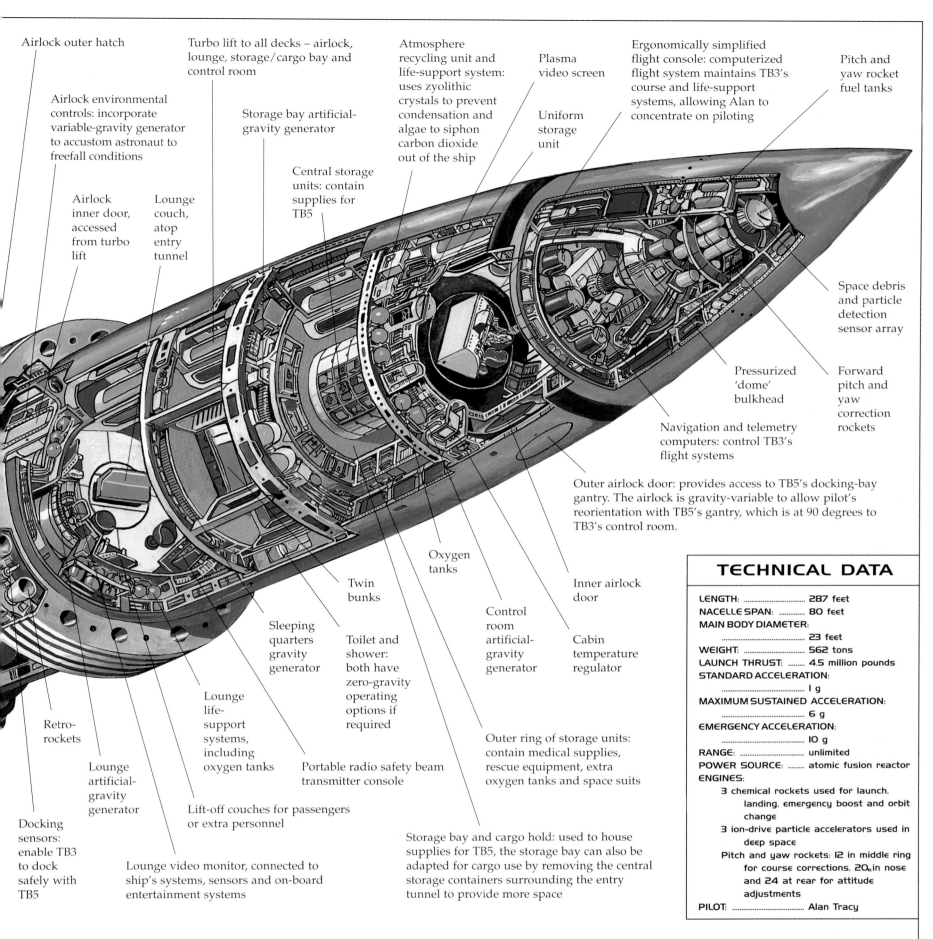

Airlock outer hatch

Turbo lift to all decks – airlock, lounge, storage/cargo bay and control room

Atmosphere recycling unit and life-support system: uses zyolithic crystals to prevent condensation and algae to siphon carbon dioxide out of the ship

Plasma video screen

Ergonomically simplified flight console: computerized flight system maintains TB3's course and life-support systems, allowing Alan to concentrate on piloting

Pitch and yaw rocket fuel tanks

Airlock environmental controls: incorporate variable-gravity generator to accustom astronaut to freefall conditions

Storage bay artificial-gravity generator

Uniform storage unit

Airlock inner door, accessed from turbo lift

Lounge couch, atop entry tunnel

Central storage units: contain supplies for TB5

Space debris and particle detection sensor array

Pressurized 'dome' bulkhead

Forward pitch and yaw correction rockets

Navigation and telemetry computers: control TB3's flight systems

Outer airlock door: provides access to TB5's docking-bay gantry. The airlock is gravity-variable to allow pilot's reorientation with TB5's gantry, which is at 90 degrees to TB3's control room.

Oxygen tanks

Inner airlock door

Twin bunks

Control room artificial-gravity generator

Sleeping quarters gravity generator

Toilet and shower: both have zero-gravity operating options if required

Cabin temperature regulator

Lounge life-support systems, including oxygen tanks

Outer ring of storage units: contain medical supplies, rescue equipment, extra oxygen tanks and space suits

Retro-rockets

Portable radio safety beam transmitter console

Lounge artificial-gravity generator

Lift-off couches for passengers or extra personnel

Docking sensors: enable TB3 to dock safely with TB5

Lounge video monitor, connected to ship's systems, sensors and on-board entertainment systems

Storage bay and cargo hold: used to house supplies for TB5, the storage bay can also be adapted for cargo use by removing the central storage containers surrounding the entry tunnel to provide more space

TECHNICAL DATA

LENGTH:	287 feet
NACELLE SPAN:	80 feet
MAIN BODY DIAMETER:	23 feet
WEIGHT:	562 tons
LAUNCH THRUST:	4.5 million pounds
STANDARD ACCELERATION:	1 g
MAXIMUM SUSTAINED ACCELERATION:	6 g
EMERGENCY ACCELERATION:	10 g
RANGE:	unlimited
POWER SOURCE:	atomic fusion reactor

ENGINES:
  3 chemical rockets used for launch, landing, emergency boost and orbit change
  3 ion-drive particle accelerators used in deep space
  Pitch and yaw rockets: 12 in middle ring for course corrections. 20 in nose and 24 at rear for attitude adjustments

PILOT:	Alan Tracy

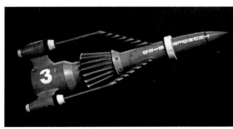

Piloted by Alan Tracy, Thunderbird 3 is the space rescue and shuttle craft of the International Rescue organization. It is launched from Tracy Island from a silo hidden under the Round House, and is often used as a shuttle to ferry supplies to Thunderbird 5. To enter the craft on Tracy Island, Alan sits on the couch in the Tracy Villa lounge. By pressing a hidden button, the couch is lowered to a waiting trolley which conveys him to TB3's launch bay. Under the base of TB3 the couch is then raised on a hydraulic ram up to the spaceship's lounge, from where Alan continues his ascent via a turbo lift to the control room. After the ram has retracted, the ship is ready for launch.

Small in comparison with the other primary International Rescue vehicles, Thunderbird 4 deals with underwater emergencies and is normally launched from Thunderbird 2's Pod 4 at the danger zone. A number of remote-controlled rescue operations can be carried out by pilot Gordon Tracy using the array of tools housed in the four forward equipment tubes. The missiles, rams, laser cutters and grabs are used to remove underwater obstacles and recover objects from the sea bed. Access to the craft is gained via the port and topside airlocks.

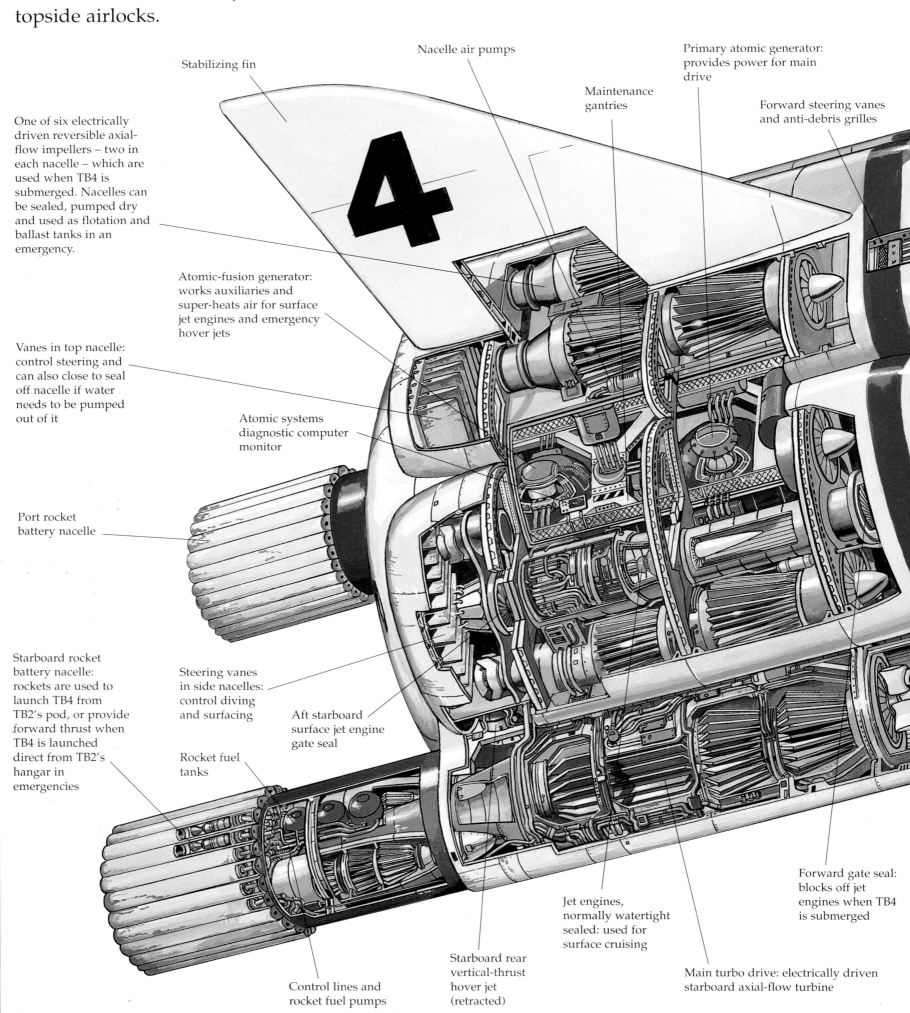

Stabilizing fin

Nacelle air pumps

Primary atomic generator: provides power for main drive

Maintenance gantries

Forward steering vanes and anti-debris grilles

One of six electrically driven reversible axial-flow impellers – two in each nacelle – which are used when TB4 is submerged. Nacelles can be sealed, pumped dry and used as flotation and ballast tanks in an emergency.

Atomic-fusion generator: works auxiliaries and super-heats air for surface jet engines and emergency hover jets

Vanes in top nacelle: control steering and can also close to seal off nacelle if water needs to be pumped out of it

Atomic systems diagnostic computer monitor

Port rocket battery nacelle

Starboard rocket battery nacelle: rockets are used to launch TB4 from TB2's pod, or provide forward thrust when TB4 is launched direct from TB2's hangar in emergencies

Steering vanes in side nacelles: control diving and surfacing

Aft starboard surface jet engine gate seal

Rocket fuel tanks

Control lines and rocket fuel pumps

Starboard rear vertical-thrust hover jet (retracted)

Jet engines, normally watertight sealed: used for surface cruising

Forward gate seal: blocks off jet engines when TB4 is submerged

Main turbo drive: electrically driven starboard axial-flow turbine

THUNDERBIRD 4

INTERNATIONAL RESCUE'S UNDERWATER RECONNAISSANCE CRAFT

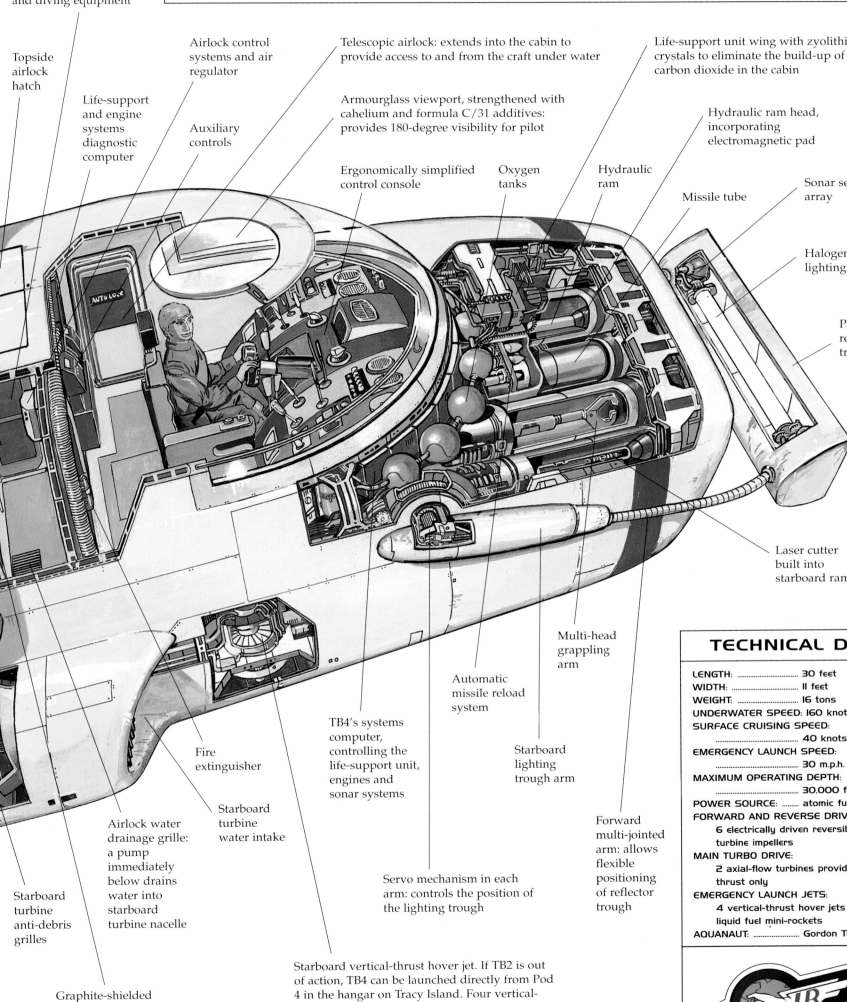

Equipment storage lockers for aqualung and diving equipment

Topside airlock hatch

Airlock control systems and air regulator

Telescopic airlock: extends into the cabin to provide access to and from the craft under water

Life-support unit wing with zyolithic crystals to eliminate the build-up of carbon dioxide in the cabin

Life-support and engine systems diagnostic computer

Auxiliary controls

Armourglass viewport, strengthened with cahelium and formula C/31 additives: provides 180-degree visibility for pilot

Hydraulic ram head, incorporating electromagnetic pad

Ergonomically simplified control console

Oxygen tanks

Hydraulic ram

Missile tube

Sonar sensor array

Halogen lighting bar

Parabolic reflector trough

Laser cutter built into starboard ram

Multi-head grappling arm

Automatic missile reload system

Starboard lighting trough arm

Fire extinguisher

TB4's systems computer, controlling the life-support unit, engines and sonar systems

Starboard turbine water intake

Forward multi-jointed arm: allows flexible positioning of reflector trough

Airlock water drainage grille: a pump immediately below drains water into starboard turbine nacelle

Servo mechanism in each arm: controls the position of the lighting trough

Starboard turbine anti-debris grilles

Graphite-shielded maintenance access hatch to atomic generators

Starboard vertical-thrust hover jet. If TB2 is out of action, TB4 can be launched directly from Pod 4 in the hangar on Tracy Island. Four vertical-thrust hover jets can convey the craft from TB2's launch bay down the runway to the shoreline. Seconds before hitting the water, the jets are retracted and sealed.

TECHNICAL DATA

LENGTH: .... 30 feet
WIDTH: .... 11 feet
WEIGHT: .... 16 tons
UNDERWATER SPEED: 160 knots
SURFACE CRUISING SPEED:
.... 40 knots
EMERGENCY LAUNCH SPEED:
.... 30 m.p.h.
MAXIMUM OPERATING DEPTH:
.... 30,000 feet
POWER SOURCE: .... atomic fusion reactor
FORWARD AND REVERSE DRIVE:
   6 electrically driven reversible axial-flow turbine impellers
MAIN TURBO DRIVE:
   2 axial-flow turbines providing forward thrust only
EMERGENCY LAUNCH JETS:
   4 vertical-thrust hover jets and 2 x 25 liquid fuel mini-rockets
AQUANAUT: .... Gordon Tracy

Vital to International Rescue's operations, Thunderbird 5 is a communications satellite located in a classified orbit around the Earth. Full monitoring of emergency calls is maintained by a series of ground stations in secret locations that relay messages to TB5 and give total coverage of the Earth's surface wherever TB5 is positioned at the time. It is manned by either John or Alan Tracy in monthly shifts, and is linked to Earth via Thunderbird 3. The satellite is electronically cloaked to avoid detection from ground-based radar or other spacecraft's sensor systems.

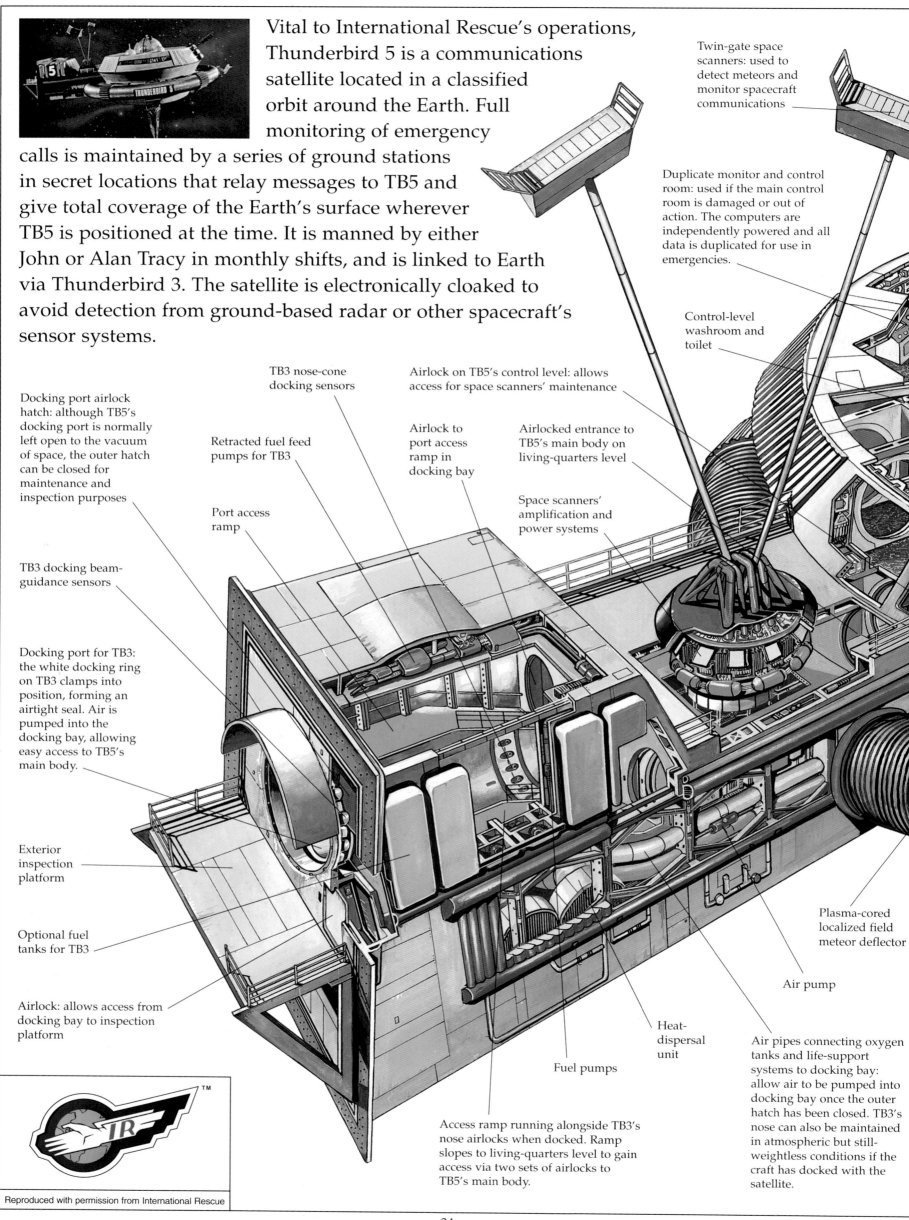

Twin-gate space scanners: used to detect meteors and monitor spacecraft communications

Duplicate monitor and control room: used if the main control room is damaged or out of action. The computers are independently powered and all data is duplicated for use in emergencies.

Control-level washroom and toilet

TB3 nose-cone docking sensors

Airlock on TB5's control level: allows access for space scanners' maintenance

Docking port airlock hatch: although TB5's docking port is normally left open to the vacuum of space, the outer hatch can be closed for maintenance and inspection purposes

Retracted fuel feed pumps for TB3

Airlock to port access ramp in docking bay

Airlocked entrance to TB5's main body on living-quarters level

Port access ramp

Space scanners' amplification and power systems

TB3 docking beam-guidance sensors

Docking port for TB3: the white docking ring on TB3 clamps into position, forming an airtight seal. Air is pumped into the docking bay, allowing easy access to TB5's main body.

Exterior inspection platform

Optional fuel tanks for TB3

Plasma-cored localized field meteor deflector

Air pump

Airlock: allows access from docking bay to inspection platform

Heat-dispersal unit

Fuel pumps

Air pipes connecting oxygen tanks and life-support systems to docking bay: allow air to be pumped into docking bay once the outer hatch has been closed. TB3's nose can also be maintained in atmospheric but still-weightless conditions if the craft has docked with the satellite.

Access ramp running alongside TB3's nose airlocks when docked. Ramp slopes to living-quarters level to gain access via two sets of airlocks to TB5's main body.

THUNDERBIRD 5

INTERNATIONAL RESCUE'S SPACE MONITORING SATELLITE

High-powered electronic telescope incorporating wide-field/planetary camera

Solar-energy panels

Emergency ladder and lift to all levels

Astrodome housing telescope and video-monitoring systems for space scanners

Access hatch from anteroom to astrodome

Medical bay

Coded-frequency antenna used for direct electronic and audiovisual communications with Tracy Island or secret relay stations

Solar panels

Space signalling laser-beam system and starfix sensors: used to maintain TB5's orbital position

Space-suit storage bay

Movable screens to cover windows from sun glare

Life-support systems control console

Orbital position-control manual override unit

TB5's control console: used to alter the satellite's position

Airlock to medical bay, stores and anteroom below astrodome, and laboratory beyond

Digital audio recorder

Plasma pumps serving the meteor deflector

Main monitor console: linked to language translating computer programs, the system selects and records all messages containing words such as 'help' and 'emergency' in all the world's languages. These messages can be automatically transferred to computer consoles throughout the station, depending where John Tracy is.

Lounge

Console linked to TB5's computer and communications systems

Life-support and power-generating systems using atomic batteries

Personal hygiene station

Field localizer magnetic-pole unit

One of six bedrooms

Oxygen tanks

Artificial-gravity generator

One of six electromagnetic 'cloaking' baffles – anti-radar systems that prevent the accidental discovery of TB5

Mobile electronic entertainment system: features a micro library of movies, TV broadcast recorder, surround music system and holographic games projection unit

Main monitoring antenna, held clear of anti-radar distortion field on long pylon

TECHNICAL DATA

LENGTH: .... 400 feet
HEIGHT (inc. antenna): 272 feet
DIAMETER (inc. meteor deflector):
.... 296 feet
WEIGHT (standard Earth gravity):
.... 976 tons
RECEPTION RANGE: ... 100 million miles
POWER: .... atomic batteries
GRAVITY:
    Previn coil artificial-gravity generator:
    Earth standard (with various options)
ORBIT:
    Geo-stationary 22,400 miles above
    the Pacific Ocean
SPACE MONITOR: .... John Tracy

CREIGHTON-WARD MANSION

THE ANCESTRAL HOME OF INTERNATIONAL RESCUE'S LONDON AGENT

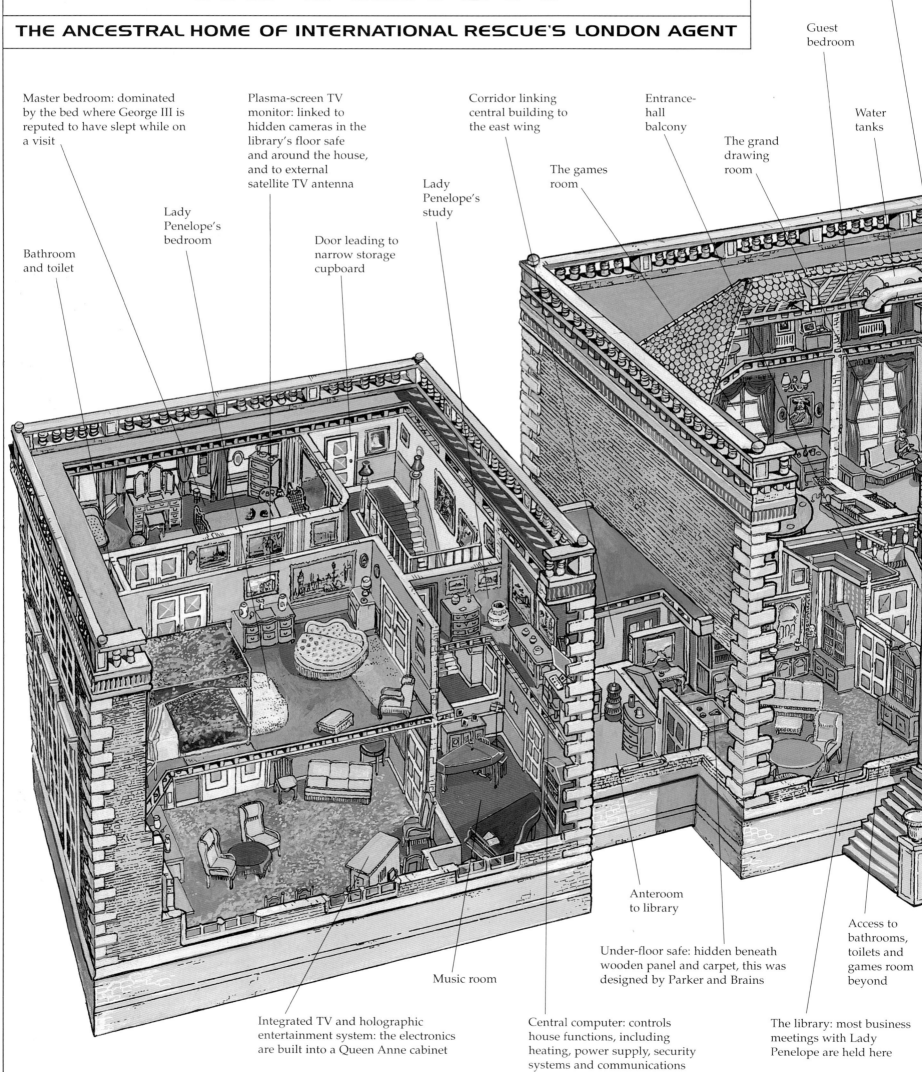

Smoke-extraction pipes

Guest bedroom

Master bedroom: dominated by the bed where George III is reputed to have slept while on a visit

Plasma-screen TV monitor: linked to hidden cameras in the library's floor safe and around the house, and to external satellite TV antenna

Corridor linking central building to the east wing

Entrance-hall balcony

Water tanks

Lady Penelope's bedroom

The grand drawing room

The games room

Lady Penelope's study

Bathroom and toilet

Door leading to narrow storage cupboard

Anteroom to library

Access to bathrooms, toilets and games room beyond

Music room

Under-floor safe: hidden beneath wooden panel and carpet, this was designed by Parker and Brains

The library: most business meetings with Lady Penelope are held here

Integrated TV and holographic entertainment system: the electronics are built into a Queen Anne cabinet

Central computer: controls house functions, including heating, power supply, security systems and communications

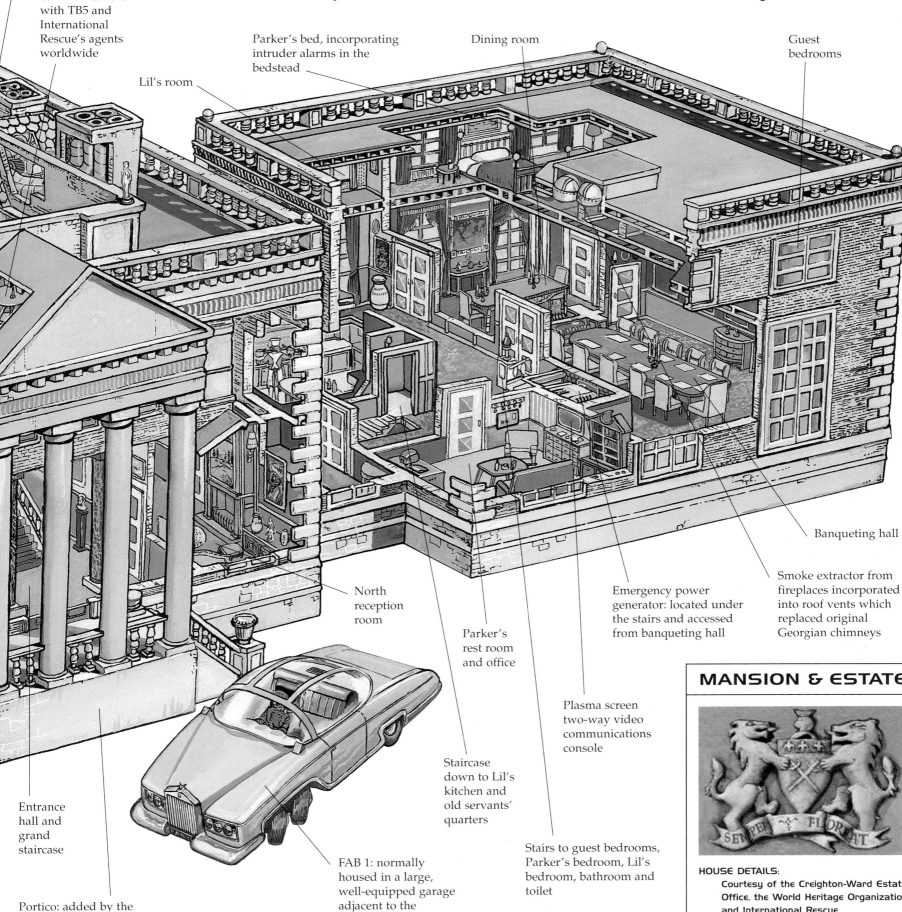

Built in 1730, the Creighton-Ward Mansion stands on the site of a Norman castle in a 2,000-acre estate at Foxleyheath, in southern England. It was designed and built in the Palladian style by Colen Campbell, the architect largely responsible for Stourhead House in Wiltshire. Designated a Grade One listed building by the World Heritage Organization, the mansion has nonetheless been altered to incorporate various burglar-alarm systems and inter-room video and audio communications, and a forensic laboratory has been built in what were the old servants' quarters.

Extractor fans: draw smoke from several fireplaces to the two remaining original chimneys on the building's roof

Satellite antenna: maintains Lady Penelope's communications with TB5 and International Rescue's agents worldwide

Lil's room

Parker's bed, incorporating intruder alarms in the bedstead

Dining room

Guest bedrooms

Banqueting hall

Smoke extractor from fireplaces incorporated into roof vents which replaced original Georgian chimneys

North reception room

Emergency power generator: located under the stairs and accessed from banqueting hall

Parker's rest room and office

Plasma screen two-way video communications console

Staircase down to Lil's kitchen and old servants' quarters

Entrance hall and grand staircase

Portico: added by the Creighton-Ward family in the nineteenth century

FAB 1: normally housed in a large, well-equipped garage adjacent to the Mansion's east wing

Stairs to guest bedrooms, Parker's bedroom, Lil's bedroom, bathroom and toilet

MANSION & ESTATE

SEMPER FLORAT

HOUSE DETAILS:
Courtesy of the Creighton-Ward Estate Office, the World Heritage Organization and International Rescue
COAT OF ARMS:
Reproduced by permission of Lady Penelope Creighton-Ward

FAB 1

LADY PENELOPE'S ROLLS-ROYCE SALOON CAR

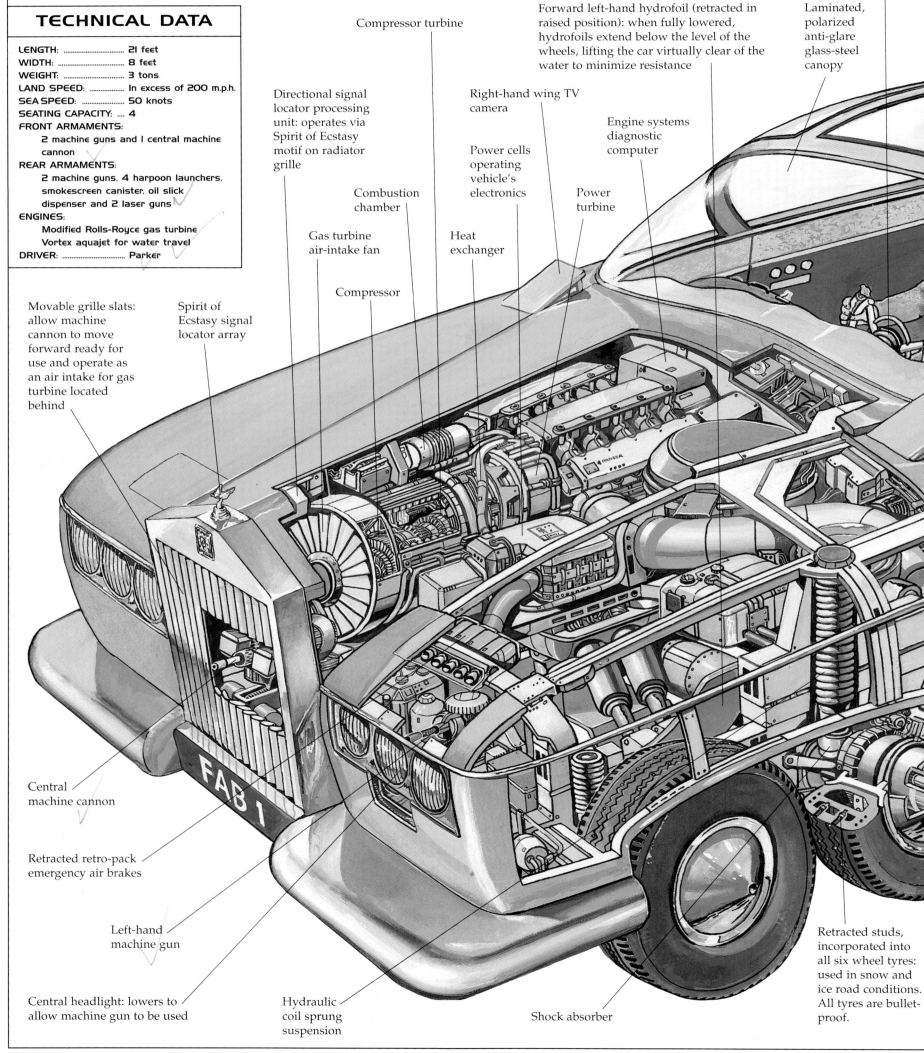

TECHNICAL DATA

LENGTH: .... 21 feet
WIDTH: .... 8 feet
WEIGHT: .... 3 tons
LAND SPEED: .... In excess of 200 m.p.h.
SEA SPEED: .... 50 knots
SEATING CAPACITY: 4
FRONT ARMAMENTS:
    2 machine guns and 1 central machine cannon
REAR ARMAMENTS:
    2 machine guns, 4 harpoon launchers, smokescreen canister, oil slick dispenser and 2 laser guns
ENGINES:
    Modified Rolls-Royce gas turbine
    Vortex aquajet for water travel
DRIVER: .... Parker

Compressor turbine

Forward left-hand hydrofoil (retracted in raised position): when fully lowered, hydrofoils extend below the level of the wheels, lifting the car virtually clear of the water to minimize resistance

Centrally placed 'power steering' wheel with air bag

Laminated, polarized anti-glare glass-steel canopy

Right-hand wing TV camera

Engine systems diagnostic computer

Directional signal locator processing unit: operates via Spirit of Ecstasy motif on radiator grille

Power cells operating vehicle's electronics

Combustion chamber

Power turbine

Gas turbine air-intake fan

Heat exchanger

Compressor

Movable grille slats: allow machine cannon to move forward ready for use and operate as an air intake for gas turbine located behind

Spirit of Ecstasy signal locator array

Central machine cannon

Retracted retro-pack emergency air brakes

Left-hand machine gun

Central headlight: lowers to allow machine gun to be used

Hydraulic coil sprung suspension

Shock absorber

Retracted studs, incorporated into all six wheel tyres: used in snow and ice road conditions. All tyres are bullet-proof.

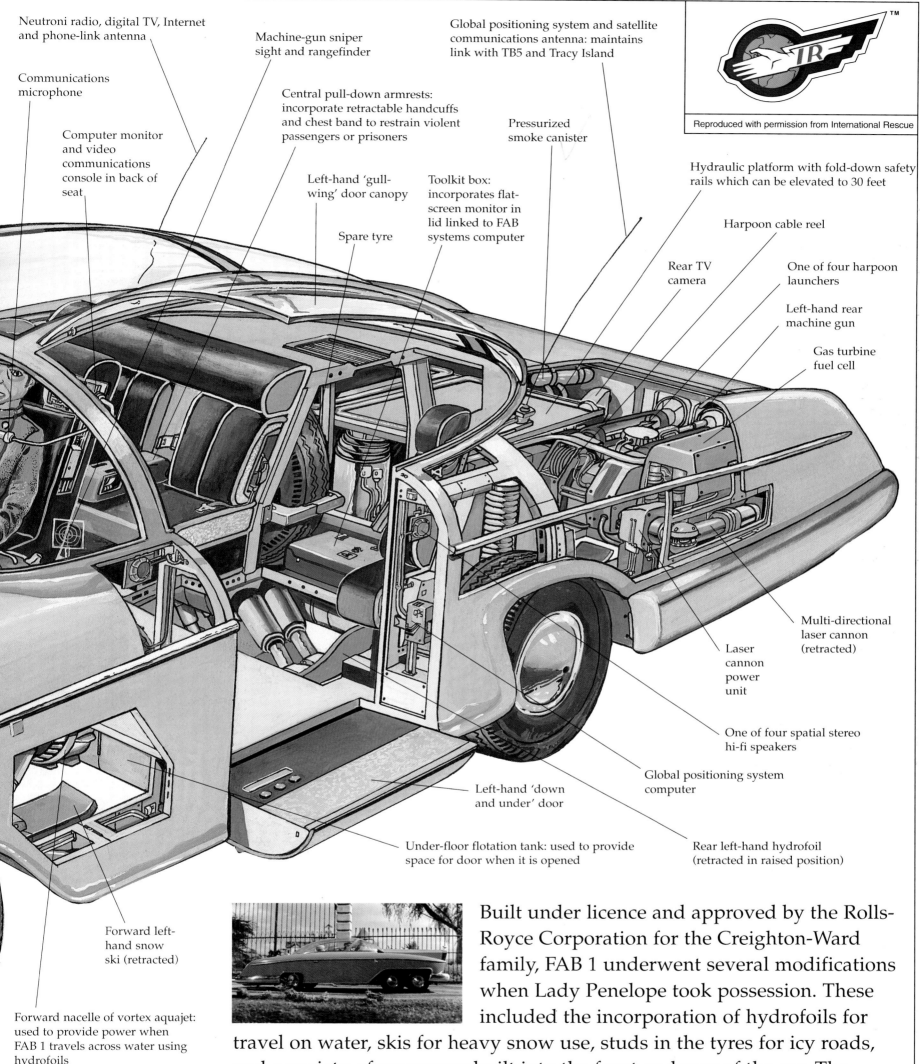

Neutroni radio, digital TV, Internet and phone-link antenna

Communications microphone

Computer monitor and video communications console in back of seat

Machine-gun sniper sight and rangefinder

Central pull-down armrests: incorporate retractable handcuffs and chest band to restrain violent passengers or prisoners

Left-hand 'gull-wing' door canopy

Toolkit box: incorporates flat-screen monitor in lid linked to FAB systems computer

Spare tyre

Global positioning system and satellite communications antenna: maintains link with TB5 and Tracy Island

Pressurized smoke canister

Hydraulic platform with fold-down safety rails which can be elevated to 30 feet

Harpoon cable reel

Rear TV camera

One of four harpoon launchers

Left-hand rear machine gun

Gas turbine fuel cell

Multi-directional laser cannon (retracted)

Laser cannon power unit

One of four spatial stereo hi-fi speakers

Global positioning system computer

Left-hand 'down and under' door

Forward left-hand snow ski (retracted)

Forward nacelle of vortex aquajet: used to provide power when FAB 1 travels across water using hydrofoils

Retracted tyre slasher, incorporated into all six wheel hubs

Under-floor flotation tank: used to provide space for door when it is opened

Rear left-hand hydrofoil (retracted in raised position)

Built under licence and approved by the Rolls-Royce Corporation for the Creighton-Ward family, FAB 1 underwent several modifications when Lady Penelope took possession. These included the incorporation of hydrofoils for travel on water, skis for heavy snow use, studs in the tyres for icy roads, and a variety of weaponry built into the front and rear of the car. The original engine was partly replaced by a Rolls-Royce-built gas turbine, giving improved performance and speeds believed to be in excess of 200 m.p.h. Many more of the modifications were carried out by International Rescue when Lady Penelope became an agent of the organization.

FAB 2

LADY PENELOPE'S PRIVATE OCEAN-GOING YACHT

FAB 2 is one of several ocean-going pleasure cruisers owned by the Creighton-Ward family. Kept in an exclusive private marina on the south coast of England, the yacht was specially built for Lady Penelope by International Engineering, a company of which Jeff Tracy is a major shareholder. FAB 2 has a top speed of 60 knots, and can be operated by either one person or up to six, depending on the duties to be performed. The yacht is mainly used for social functions when Lady Penelope is travelling but can also function as a floating operations control centre for International Rescue if required.

Ergonomically simplified control console: allows FAB 2 to be controlled by the central computer so single crew member can steer

Engineering and yacht's systems monitor

Search-light

Barometric pressure sensor

Bridge

Storage locker: contains life buoys, life jackets and signal beacons

Video and communications plasma screen

Starboard access to promenade deck

Air-conditioning vent

Foredeck access hatch

Video phone

Bar

Access steps to foredeck

Forward lounge

Emergency towing cleat

Laundry room

Toilet

Water purification, filtration and sanitation plant

Fused titanium-alloy double-walled hull

Sonar system computerized control unit and torpedo guidance system

Retractable sonar array

Dual starboard torpedo tubes

Port anchor

Inner torpedo tube hatch hydraulics system

Torpedo loading bay

Central corridor

Bedroom used by Lil if she is travelling with Lady Penelope

Underside video cameras: protected in a transparent cahelium-bonded dome, twin video cameras with powerful lights can be lowered through the keel access hatch to monitor any activity beneath the yacht

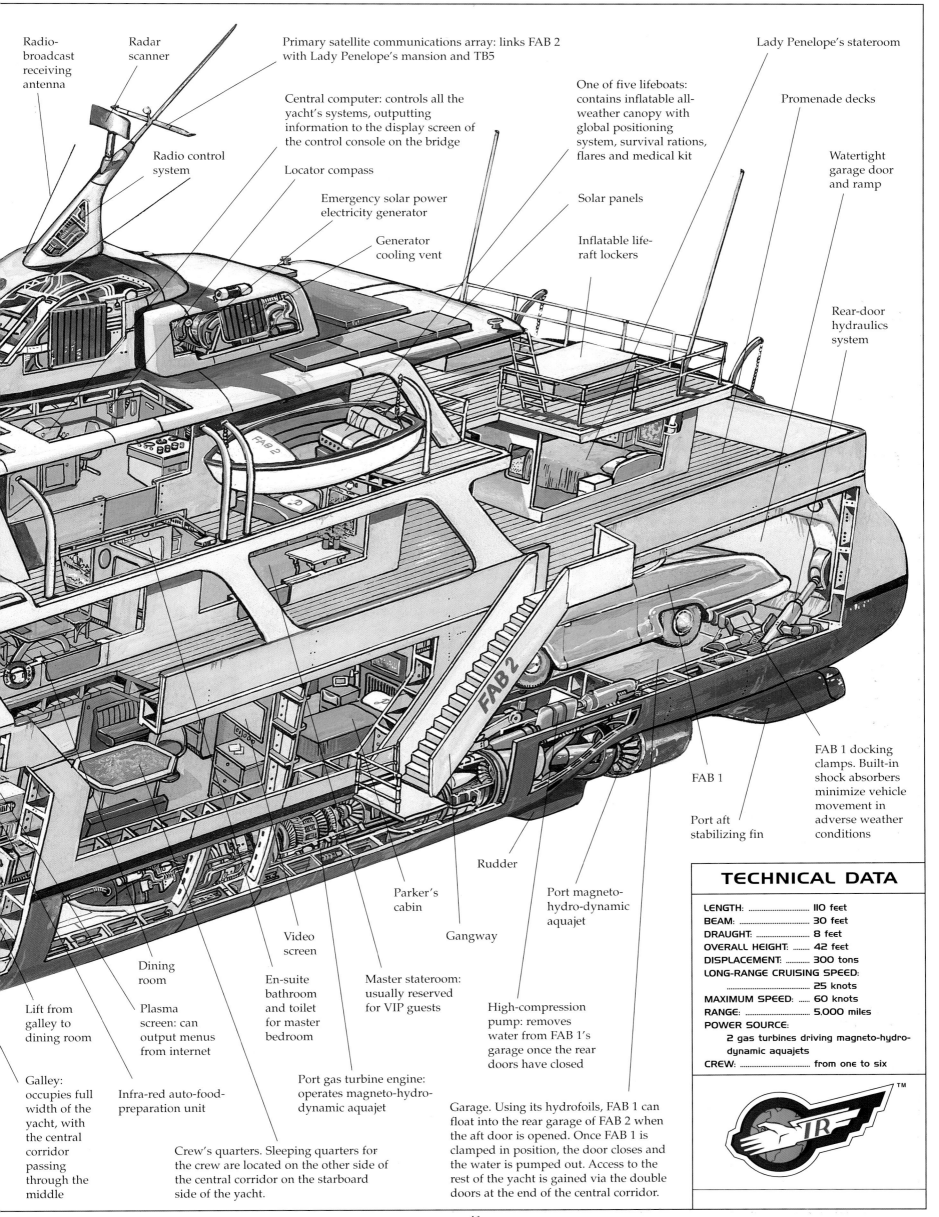

Radio-broadcast receiving antenna

Radar scanner

Radio control system

Primary satellite communications array: links FAB 2 with Lady Penelope's mansion and TB5

Central computer: controls all the yacht's systems, outputting information to the display screen of the control console on the bridge

Locator compass

Emergency solar power electricity generator

Generator cooling vent

Lady Penelope's stateroom

One of five lifeboats: contains inflatable all-weather canopy with global positioning system, survival rations, flares and medical kit

Promenade decks

Solar panels

Inflatable life-raft lockers

Watertight garage door and ramp

Rear-door hydraulics system

FAB 1 docking clamps. Built-in shock absorbers minimize vehicle movement in adverse weather conditions

FAB 1

Port aft stabilizing fin

Rudder

Port magneto-hydro-dynamic aquajet

Parker's cabin

Gangway

Video screen

Dining room

Plasma screen: can output menus from internet

En-suite bathroom and toilet for master bedroom

Master stateroom: usually reserved for VIP guests

High-compression pump: removes water from FAB 1's garage once the rear doors have closed

Lift from galley to dining room

Galley: occupies full width of the yacht, with the central corridor passing through the middle

Infra-red auto-food-preparation unit

Port gas turbine engine: operates magneto-hydro-dynamic aquajet

Crew's quarters. Sleeping quarters for the crew are located on the other side of the central corridor on the starboard side of the yacht.

Garage. Using its hydrofoils, FAB 1 can float into the rear garage of FAB 2 when the aft door is opened. Once FAB 1 is clamped in position, the door closes and the water is pumped out. Access to the rest of the yacht is gained via the double doors at the end of the central corridor.

TECHNICAL DATA

LENGTH:	110 feet
BEAM:	30 feet
DRAUGHT:	8 feet
OVERALL HEIGHT:	42 feet
DISPLACEMENT:	300 tons
LONG-RANGE CRUISING SPEED:	25 knots
MAXIMUM SPEED:	60 knots
RANGE:	5,000 miles
POWER SOURCE:	2 gas turbines driving magneto-hydro-dynamic aquajets
CREW:	from one to six

SUN PROBE

THE SUN PROBE MISSION AND OTHER SPACECRAFT RESCUES

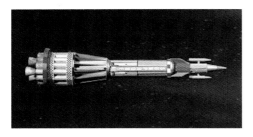

The Sun Probe mission would have been a disaster but for International Rescue. Using an ion drive and a chemical rocket system, the Sun Probe's launch thrust of 20 million pounds gave it the acceleration to reach solar orbit in a week. Three solarnauts remained aboard while the nose-cone probe was launched to collect particles from a solar prominence and then retrieved. But high radiation levels meant the Sun Probe's retros failed. Even Cape Kennedy's back-up system couldn't stop the ship heading straight for the sun. A radio safety beam activated from Thunderbird 3 eventually fired the retros, allowing the Sun Probe and its occupants to return home safely.

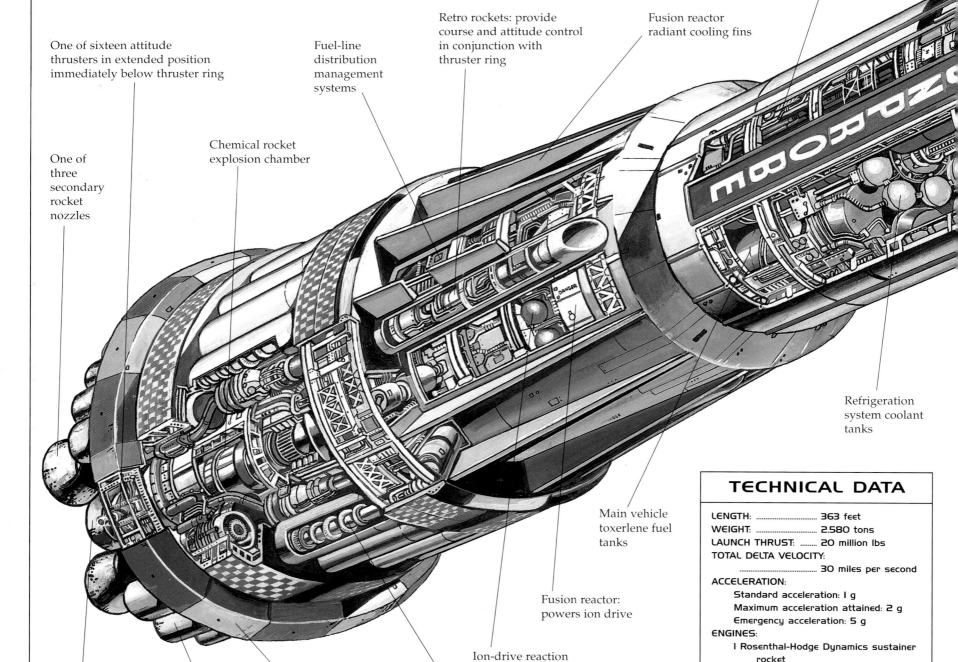

One of sixteen attitude thrusters in extended position immediately below thruster ring

One of three secondary rocket nozzles

Chemical rocket explosion chamber

Fuel-line distribution management systems

Retro rockets: provide course and attitude control in conjunction with thruster ring

Fusion reactor radiant cooling fins

Toxerlene fuel management system modules

Toxerlene fuel lines: connect fuel tanks to main chemical rockets and attitude thrusters

Refrigeration system coolant tanks

Main vehicle toxerlene fuel tanks

Fusion reactor: powers ion drive

Ion-drive reaction mass tanks

Main sustainer chemical rocket nozzle

Ion-drive exhaust vents

Attitude thruster ring

Ion-drive particle accelerator

TECHNICAL DATA

LENGTH:	363 feet
WEIGHT:	2,580 tons
LAUNCH THRUST:	20 million lbs
TOTAL DELTA VELOCITY:	30 miles per second
ACCELERATION:	
Standard acceleration: 1 g	
Maximum acceleration attained: 2 g	
Emergency acceleration: 5 g	
ENGINES:	
1 Rosenthal-Hodge Dynamics sustainer rocket	
3 Rosenthal-Hodge Dynamics secondary rockets	
4 retro rockets	
16 attitude thrusters	
FUEL:	Toxerlene
ION DRIVE:	24 Amalgamated Atomics Inc. TE-14 thrust modules

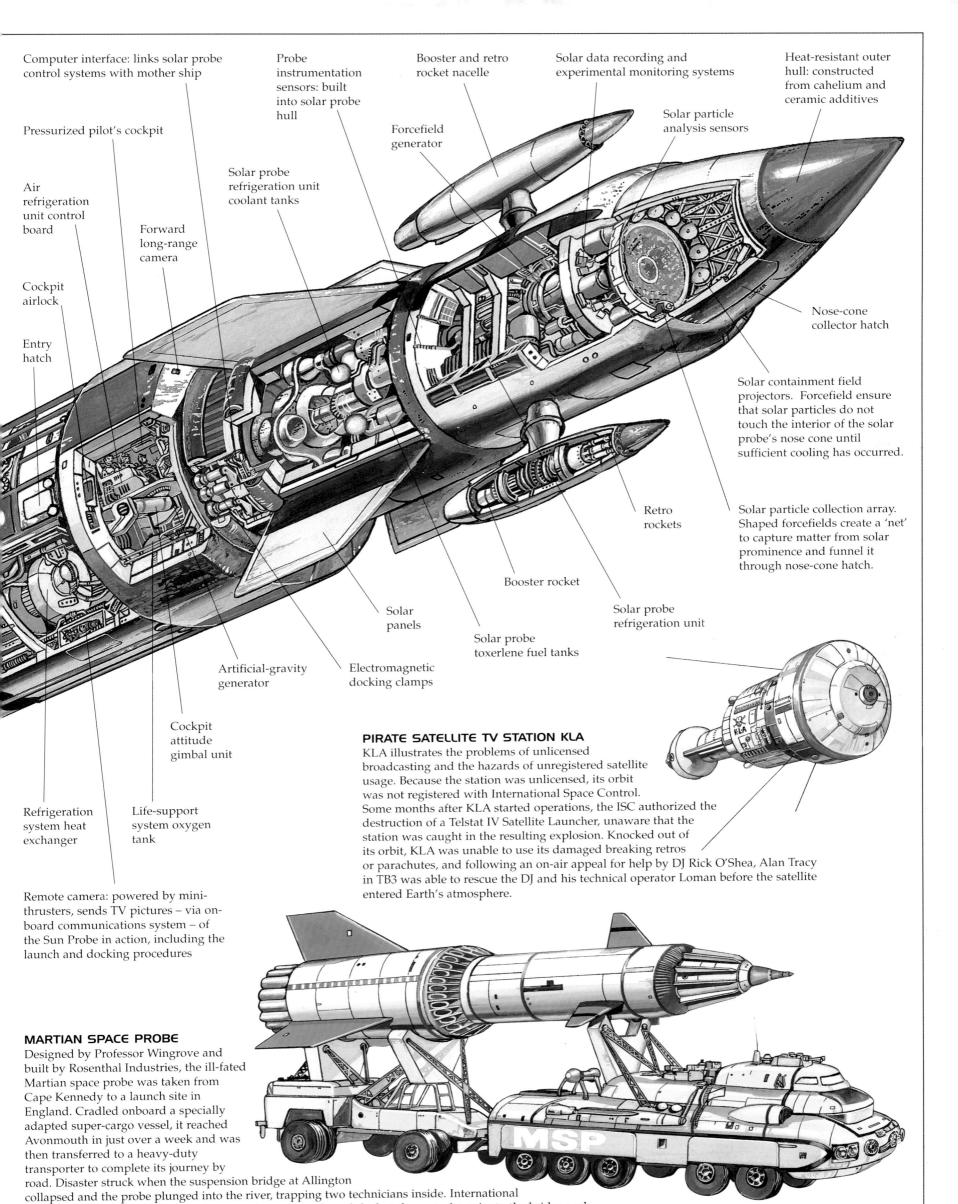

Computer interface: links solar probe control systems with mother ship

Probe instrumentation sensors: built into solar probe hull

Booster and retro rocket nacelle

Solar data recording and experimental monitoring systems

Heat-resistant outer hull: constructed from cahelium and ceramic additives

Pressurized pilot's cockpit

Forcefield generator

Solar particle analysis sensors

Air refrigeration unit control board

Solar probe refrigeration unit coolant tanks

Forward long-range camera

Cockpit airlock

Nose-cone collector hatch

Entry hatch

Solar containment field projectors. Forcefield ensure that solar particles do not touch the interior of the solar probe's nose cone until sufficient cooling has occurred.

Retro rockets

Solar particle collection array. Shaped forcefields create a 'net' to capture matter from solar prominence and funnel it through nose-cone hatch.

Solar panels

Booster rocket

Solar probe refrigeration unit

Solar probe toxerlene fuel tanks

Artificial-gravity generator

Electromagnetic docking clamps

Cockpit attitude gimbal unit

Refrigeration system heat exchanger

Life-support system oxygen tank

PIRATE SATELLITE TV STATION KLA

KLA illustrates the problems of unlicensed broadcasting and the hazards of unregistered satellite usage. Because the station was unlicensed, its orbit was not registered with International Space Control. Some months after KLA started operations, the ISC authorized the destruction of a Telstat IV Satellite Launcher, unaware that the station was caught in the resulting explosion. Knocked out of its orbit, KLA was unable to use its damaged breaking retros or parachutes, and following an on-air appeal for help by DJ Rick O'Shea, Alan Tracy in TB3 was able to rescue the DJ and his technical operator Loman before the satellite entered Earth's atmosphere.

Remote camera: powered by mini-thrusters, sends TV pictures – via on-board communications system – of the Sun Probe in action, including the launch and docking procedures

MARTIAN SPACE PROBE

Designed by Professor Wingrove and built by Rosenthal Industries, the ill-fated Martian space probe was taken from Cape Kennedy to a launch site in England. Cradled onboard a specially adapted super-cargo vessel, it reached Avonmouth in just over a week and was then transferred to a heavy-duty transporter to complete its journey by road. Disaster struck when the suspension bridge at Allington collapsed and the probe plunged into the river, trapping two technicians inside. International Rescue was able to save them and recover the command module, but the cost of repairs to the bridge and the loss of the rocket bankrupted Rosenthal Industries and put an end to the Martian space probe project.

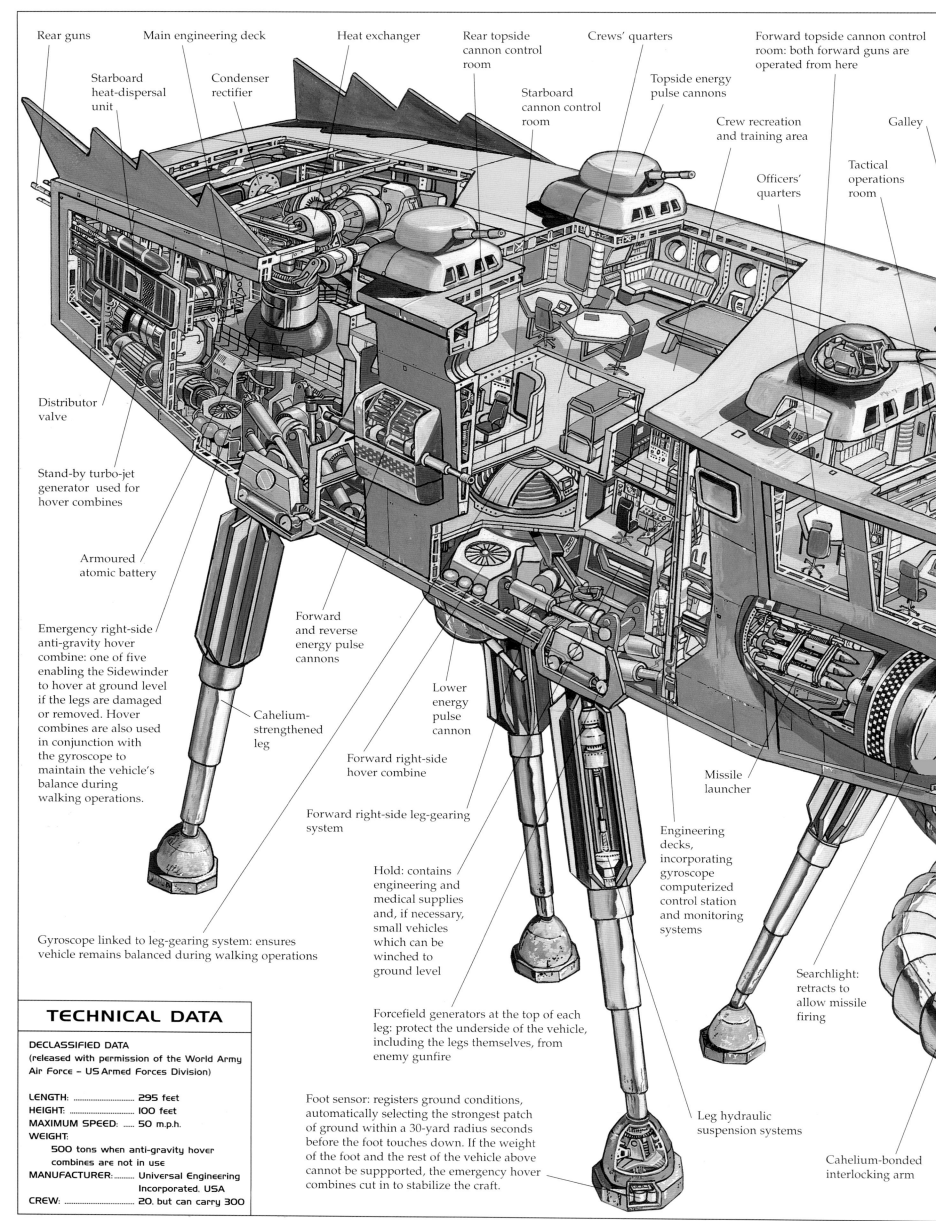

Rear guns

Main engineering deck

Heat exchanger

Rear topside cannon control room

Crews' quarters

Forward topside cannon control room: both forward guns are operated from here

Starboard heat-dispersal unit

Condenser rectifier

Starboard cannon control room

Topside energy pulse cannons

Crew recreation and training area

Galley

Officers' quarters

Tactical operations room

Distributor valve

Stand-by turbo-jet generator used for hover combines

Armoured atomic battery

Emergency right-side anti-gravity hover combine: one of five enabling the Sidewinder to hover at ground level if the legs are damaged or removed. Hover combines are also used in conjunction with the gyroscope to maintain the vehicle's balance during walking operations.

Forward and reverse energy pulse cannons

Cahelium-strengthened leg

Lower energy pulse cannon

Forward right-side hover combine

Forward right-side leg-gearing system

Missile launcher

Engineering decks, incorporating gyroscope computerized control station and monitoring systems

Gyroscope linked to leg-gearing system: ensures vehicle remains balanced during walking operations

Hold: contains engineering and medical supplies and, if necessary, small vehicles which can be winched to ground level

Forcefield generators at the top of each leg: protect the underside of the vehicle, including the legs themselves, from enemy gunfire

Searchlight: retracts to allow missile firing

Leg hydraulic suspension systems

Cahelium-bonded interlocking arm

Foot sensor: registers ground conditions, automatically selecting the strongest patch of ground within a 30-yard radius seconds before the foot touches down. If the weight of the foot and the rest of the vehicle above cannot be suppported, the emergency hover combines cut in to stabilize the craft.

TECHNICAL DATA

DECLASSIFIED DATA
(released with permission of the World Army
Air Force – US Armed Forces Division)

LENGTH: .... 295 feet
HEIGHT: .... 100 feet
MAXIMUM SPEED: ...... 50 m.p.h.
WEIGHT:
    500 tons when anti-gravity hover
    combines are not in use
MANUFACTURER: .... Universal Engineering
                        Incorporated, USA
CREW: .... 20, but can carry 300

SIDEWINDER

US ARMY JUNGLE CAT CLASS ALL-TERRAIN TRANSPORT VEHICLE

Plasma screen: displays maps, vehicle system diagnostics, video communications and Internet data

One of International Rescue's early missions involved a prototype Sidewinder, an all-terrain transport vehicle commissioned by the US Army. Several improvements have been made to the twenty production versions now in use, primarily in jungles worldwide. Built by Universal Engineering Incorporated, the gyroscopically balanced Sidewinders can clear whole areas of jungle, creating landing sites for helijets and troop-carrying aircraft. Improvements made since the initial (and potentially disastrous) prototype tests include the addition of emergency vertical-thrust hover combines that stabilize the progress of the machine through rough terrain and stop it sinking into soft or unstable ground.

Topside emergency exit hatch

Satellite communications antenna

Emergency ladder to all levels

Control room with ergonomically simplified control console: three crew members minimum

Forward searchlight

Pincer distance triangulation sensor

Pincers incorporating cahelium-strengthened 'teeth'

Centrally placed forward vertical-thrust hover combine

Lift to all levels: system incorporates telescopic tube, allowing lift to descend to ground level

Multi-band sensor arrays behind forward searchlights: detect radiation and heat and measure atmospheric conditions. The system also calculates distances between the front of the vehicle and objects in its path, in conjunction with the sensors on each pincer.

Primary forcefield generators: placed behind forward search lights and sensor arrays

Interlocking arm and pincer control system

Laser cutters incorporated within central opening of pincer

CRABLOGGER

INTERNATIONAL ROBOTICS' FOREST-CLEARANCE MACHINE

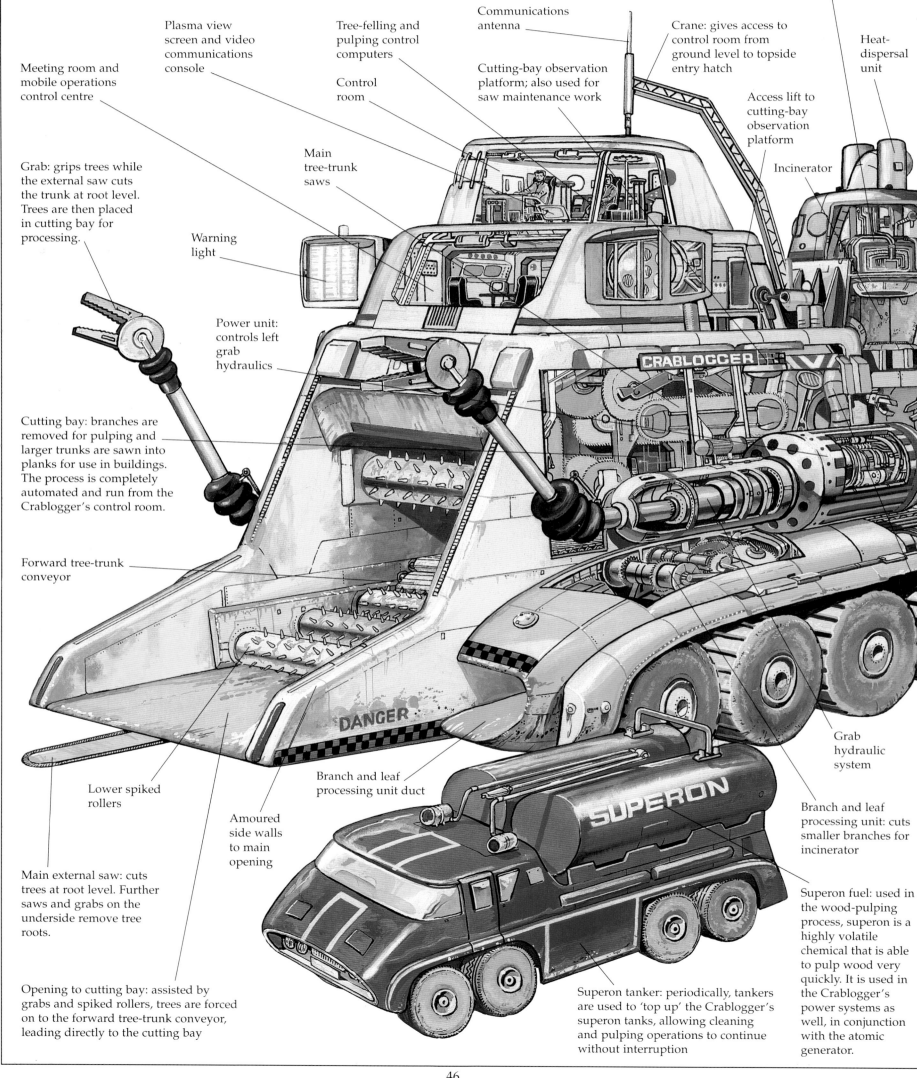

Atomic plant: supplies power to the Crablogger's drive turbines and incinerator

Communications antenna

Plasma view screen and video communications console

Tree-felling and pulping control computers

Crane: gives access to control room from ground level to topside entry hatch

Heat-dispersal unit

Meeting room and mobile operations control centre

Control room

Cutting-bay observation platform; also used for saw maintenance work

Access lift to cutting-bay observation platform

Main tree-trunk saws

Incinerator

Grab: grips trees while the external saw cuts the trunk at root level. Trees are then placed in cutting bay for processing.

Warning light

Power unit: controls left grab hydraulics

Cutting bay: branches are removed for pulping and larger trunks are sawn into planks for use in buildings. The process is completely automated and run from the Crablogger's control room.

Forward tree-trunk conveyor

Grab hydraulic system

Lower spiked rollers

Branch and leaf processing unit duct

Branch and leaf processing unit: cuts smaller branches for incinerator

Amoured side walls to main opening

Main external saw: cuts trees at root level. Further saws and grabs on the underside remove tree roots.

Superon fuel: used in the wood-pulping process, superon is a highly volatile chemical that is able to pulp wood very quickly. It is used in the Crablogger's power systems as well, in conjunction with the atomic generator.

Opening to cutting bay: assisted by grabs and spiked rollers, trees are forced on to the forward tree-trunk conveyor, leading directly to the cutting bay

Superon tanker: periodically, tankers are used to 'top up' the Crablogger's superon tanks, allowing cleaning and pulping operations to continue without interruption

Built to order by International Robotics, the Crablogger series of forest-clearing machines has proved to be a fast and effective way of preparing forest areas for road-building schemes. Divided in two, the front section cuts and uproots trees, sawing the trunks into planks and incinerating leaves. Planks are passed through to the back section, where they are either stored for collection – and then used in the building industry – or, together with larger branches, pulped for later use in industries such as paper-making. In the early years of the twenty-first century, a global ban on rainforest destruction was introduced. Crabloggers operate on the basis that felled trees must be replaced elsewhere, maintaining a worldwide balance and possible growth of forest areas.

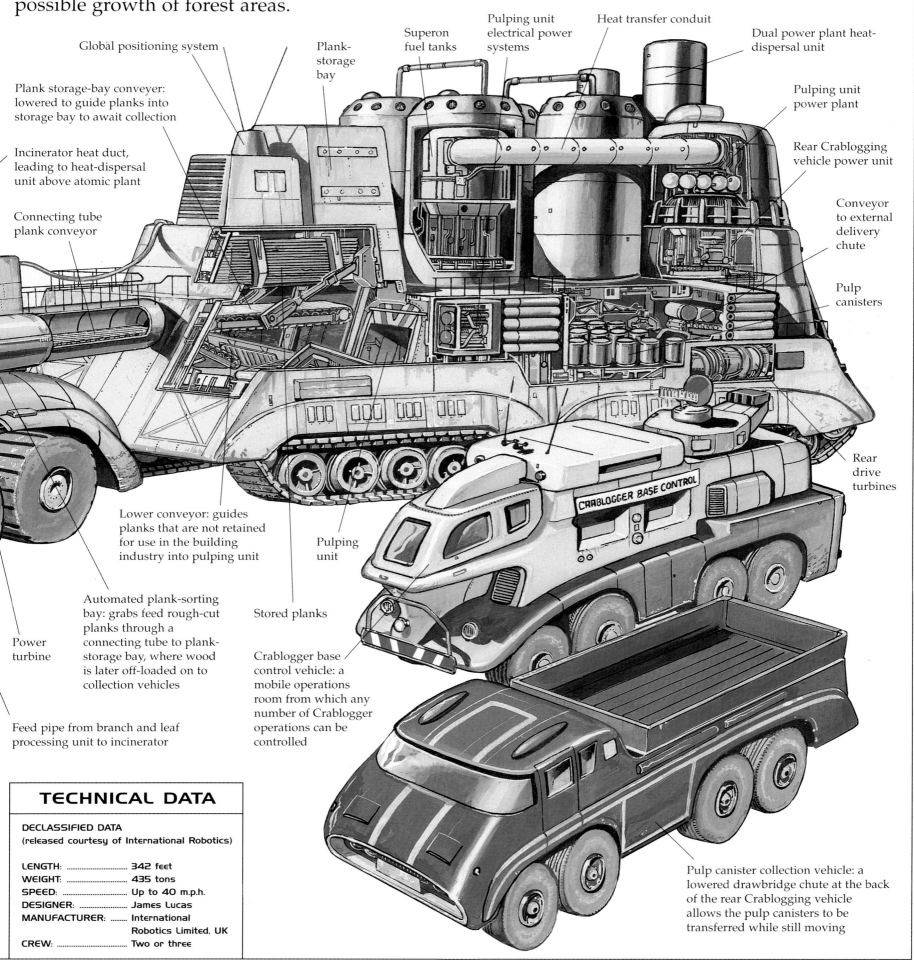

Global positioning system

Plank storage-bay conveyer: lowered to guide planks into storage bay to await collection

Incinerator heat duct, leading to heat-dispersal unit above atomic plant

Connecting tube plank conveyor

Plank-storage bay

Superon fuel tanks

Pulping unit electrical power systems

Heat transfer conduit

Dual power plant heat-dispersal unit

Pulping unit power plant

Rear Crablogging vehicle power unit

Conveyor to external delivery chute

Pulp canisters

Rear drive turbines

Lower conveyor: guides planks that are not retained for use in the building industry into pulping unit

Pulping unit

Automated plank-sorting bay: grabs feed rough-cut planks through a connecting tube to plank-storage bay, where wood is later off-loaded on to collection vehicles

Stored planks

Crablogger base control vehicle: a mobile operations room from which any number of Crablogger operations can be controlled

Power turbine

Feed pipe from branch and leaf processing unit to incinerator

CRABLOGGER BASE CONTROL

Pulp canister collection vehicle: a lowered drawbridge chute at the back of the rear Crablogging vehicle allows the pulp canisters to be transferred while still moving

TECHNICAL DATA

DECLASSIFIED DATA
(released courtesy of International Robotics)

LENGTH:	342 feet
WEIGHT:	435 tons
SPEED:	Up to 40 m.p.h.
DESIGNER:	James Lucas
MANUFACTURER:	International Robotics Limited, UK
CREW:	Two or three

ALSO AVAILABLE:

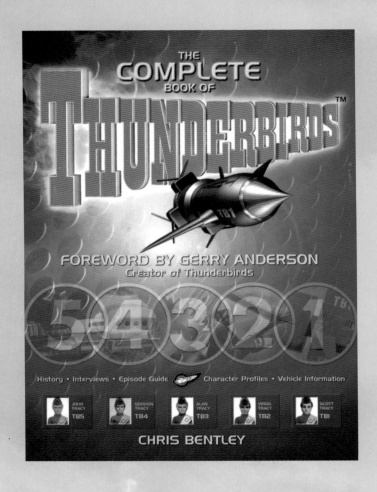

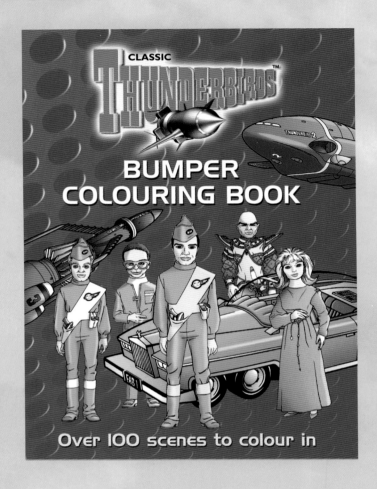

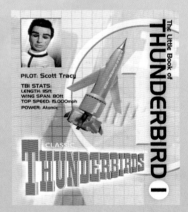

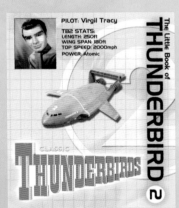

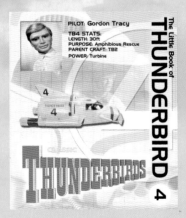

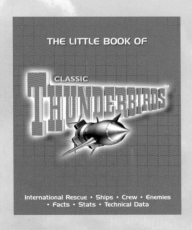